# Loving Life after Sixty

# Loving
# Life
*after*
# Sixty

*Celebrating the Autumn of Your Life*

By Tom Paugh

**Willow Creek PRESS**

MINOCQUA, WISCONSIN

Additional copyrights and credits are on page 6.

Published by Willow Creek Press
P.O. Box 147
Minocqua, Wisconsin 54548

For information on other Willow Creek titles, call 1-800-850-9453.

*Library of Congress Cataloging-in-Publication Data*
Paugh, Tom.
     Loving life after sixty : celebrating the autumn of your life / by Tom Paugh.
          p.     cm.
     ISBN   1-57223-283-8
     1. Aged Life skills guides. 2. Old age--Philosophy.   I. Title.   II. Title: Loving life after sixty.

HQ1061.P335   1999
305.26--dc21
                                                                                          99-31679
                                                                                               CIP

Printed in the U.S.A.

# CREDITS

My grateful thanks to all who graciously consented to give permission to be quoted. Obviously, all quotes used added depth, humor and/or insight to the subjects at hand.

—T.P.

# CONTENTS

# ACKNOWLEDGMENTS

*A person who publishes a book willfully appears
before the populace with his pants down.*
—EDNA ST. VINCENT MILLAY (1892-1950)

Like the figure locked inside the unmolded block of clay, early
on this book was little more than a shapeless blob in my
mind. I was not at all sure what it was I was writing, but I
figured if I could get enough words on paper then perhaps,
being an editor by trade, I could pick and choose and re-
arrange and find some sort of meaning amid chaos. This book,
that began as another book entirely—a monstrous book that
can only be described as "The Book of Everything"—had to
be taken apart and reassembled, some parts discarded, some
retained and still others set aside for other projects.

I recalled the advice of my long ago writing hero, Mr. E.
Hemingway, who had made the seemingly obvious suggestion
that a writer should write on subjects he knows something
about. Well, I had put in my years and what I for sure knew
something about was being over sixty and those were the
words I saved and then added to. The result, with the following help, is this modest volume.

From the beginning to the end of the writing process my
wife Anne encouraged, advised and endured. She read the
trials, the errors and the results. Her moral support and

substantive suggestions kept me going and greatly enhanced the final product.

Nick Lyons was the first professional to read my very rough early attempts. He offered his insightful suggestions without strings, a friend helping out a friend and at that point I truly needed help. His early encouragement and advice made me feel that there might actually be a book in my future.

Others who made suggestions and offered help were Zack Taylor, Jody Mullins, James Branch, Nell Doland, Reed and Judy Hoisington, Ila Kittle, Jennifer Kopp, Tom Vincent, Lorraine and Ted Kesting. Thanks to Kit and George Harrison for suggesting their own publisher, Willow Creek Press, to me for this book. And thanks also to Tom Petrie, Publisher of Willow Creek Press, for saying yes.

Greetings, salutations and regards to the two dozen people I wrote my "Letters Never Sent" to. Those of you among the living know who you are . . . and you owe me a letter.

And, finally, to the many sages, writers, poets, song lyricists and other famous and not so famous men and women whose quotes I have selected to embellish each chapter, I offer my deepest respects and humble thanks (see credits). You not only said it better, you said it first.

*I grow old . . . I grow old . . .*
*I shall wear the bottoms of my trousers rolled.*
—T.S. ELLIOT *The Love Song of J. Alfred Prufrock* (1917)

# INTRODUCTION

*To enter the country of old age is a new experience, different from what you supposed it to be. Nobody, man or woman, knows the country until he has lived in it and has taken out his citizenship papers.*

—MALCOLM CAWLEY (1898-1989)

At sixty-plus, your back may ache, your breath may be short, but it's what you think about that really counts. This text is by no means your standard self-help treatise, but reading all of it or just some of it may enable you to re-evaluate where you are in your life, and where you want to go.

In deciding to write what turned out to be this book, I was at least partially motivated by the faint hope that I might raise the level of respect in which I was held by members of my family and close friends. I was sixty-eight years old and retired and good for taking out the garbage, mowing the lawn and squandering my pension money on things everybody else needed. I was a competent baby sitter and always available because at my age what else did I have to do? Perhaps I missed, just a tiny bit, the former deference accorded to a busy person doing "important things."

So when I made my announcement to family members that I was seriously writing a book and no longer just piddling on the computer, I would like to report that my status immediately elevated. It did not. Nevertheless, write I did, and ever so slowly the pages mounted up and after a while I had enough to send off to a publisher for a look see. Did I now sense more family respect? Not really. But, the way I felt about myself was undergoing a change. I was actually occupied again doing something, well, if not exactly "important" at least viable and visible; by my own efforts I had produced a stack of white paper sheets covered with words. Whether or not the stack would ever turn out to be a real book in a real bookstore was not as important as the fact that I had never had a happier period during my four years of retirement. I plan to keep on working at this machine because it fills me with a sense of purpose and because trying to arrange thoughts on paper has helped me know more about myself, more about how I feel, what I think; more about the life I have lived and am living. Hopefully reading them can do the same for you.

The quotes that appear throughout reveal how others have expressed themselves on the various subjects under scrutiny. A good deal of research has gone into this area. Paging through newspapers, magazines, books, song lyrics, and other source materials I have been (and you will be) exposed to the succinct thoughts of man through the ages. I discovered that the most written about subject seems to be death, possibly indicating that people prefer to pontificate about things they do not really understand. We know about dying—too much about dying—but death and after death are subjects about which we humans can only have opinions, speculations and beliefs.

I was also struck by the repeated variations on a variety of life enlightening themes from the earliest thinkers to today's ponderers and pundits. Over and over they (we) think and re-think the big questions of life, death, love, happiness, sex, sorrow, heaven and Earth. As long as humans have existed and will exist we have been, will be, looking at and trying to re-think and re-express ourselves on these imponderables.

Those of us who have attained the age of sixty years or more need to think about the big questions of life and arrive at our own conclusions and positions both for peace of mind and self enlightenment. As individuals we have choices to make unless we wish to expire not having seriously considered our place in the overall scheme of things. It is my hope that this book may be of some help to each reader in that regard. The Seven Sages (c. 650-c. 590 BC.) advised, "Know thyself." Certainly that is the best place to begin in any quest for enlightenment because until we understand something of ourselves, how can we possibly begin to understand our neighbors much less why we're here and what it might be all about?

Just a note about the nursery rhymes that launch each chapter. These often nonsensical bits of anonymous poetry and doggerel have been with us for centuries. The title "Mother Goose" was first published by Charles Perrault in 1697 and was a collection of these traditional bits of patter which until then had been passed down mostly by word of mouth. Why run them here? Because life is full of mystery and humor and many things cannot be explained in straight forward fashion. So I have tried to start off each chapter with a curious smile to ease us into our consideration of some of life's deeper meanings:

> *Three blind mice,*
> *Baked in a pie,*
> *With silver bells and cockle shells.*

*But never to be eaten because,*
*Of course,*
*The dish ran away with the spoon.*

This is apropos of nothing, except that so often life is crazy, mixed up and seems to have no meaning.

The "Letters Never Sent" at the end of each chapter are to certain people I have known who came to mind as I considered various subjects. Strange to write letters to friends long out of touch or dead, but I found it somehow liberating. I discovered I now miss them all, the loved and the unloved. Come on back old friends and enemies; let's get it on one more time.

*You don't write a book to tell what you know;*
*you write a book to find out what you know.*

—Lawrence Shames, "Sunburn" (1995)

# RETIREMENT

*There was a jolly miller once,*
*Lived on the River Dee;*
*He worked and sang from morn till night,*
*No lark more blithe than he.*
*And this the burden of his song*
*Forever used to be:*
*I care for nobody, no not I,*
*If nobody cares for me.*

(Here is a miller obviously ripe for retirement.)

A t sixty you may be sailing along pretty good, riding the peak of your intellectual powers and earning more money than at any time in your past. Life by all outward appearances is good, but there probably is lurking in your subconscience the realization that everything will not continue on this up-curve forever. History dictates that at some ever-nearing future point changes await—changes that can arrive with startling suddenness. Preparations must be made.

*Cessation of work is not accompanied by cessation of expenses.*
——CATO THE ELDER, "De Agri Cultura" (2nd c. B.C.)

By this time the word "benefits" as in "pension plan"
should have emerged into the forefront of your conscious-
ness. But, frankly, sixty is way late for arranging one's financial security in retirement. These pages will offer no magic
formula for those sixty-year-olds who have not been using
IRA's, Keogh plans, pension plans, money funds, stock and
bond markets, gold coins, real estate ventures, art works
and other various means of saving and growing money. I
don't mean to indicate that you need to be rich, but you do
require sufficient income to be comfortable. If you have
been neglectful, however, you may now wish to consider
the possibility of extending your career another few years
with the objective of correcting your past financial over-
sights. Even part-time work might satisfy your needs. There
should still be plenty of time.

*Let me tell you about the very rich.*
*They are different from you and me.*
——F. SCOTT FITZGERALD, "The Rich Boy" (1926)

On the other hand if you have been unusually successful and have already collected enough for a secure financial future, you may wish to take early retirement. A trip around the world may well be easier and more enjoyable at sixty than seventy.

*When you do a job long enough, you sort of become the job. But, when you can no longer do the job, then what do you become?*

—*CYBLE* (TV show 1995)

The merry-go-round comes to a screeching halt: the end! You leave your former place of work, perhaps never to return. There remains only a gaping emptiness and your apprehension grows as you contemplate this new void. A grim view presents itself—all that remains of my life is nothingness, and then death. This feeling should soon pass. All of us have been conditioned throughout our lives to begin, to end and then to begin again. From infancy we crawl, we toddle, we walk, we gurgle, we talk, we go to pre-school, kindergarten, grade school, high school, college. We move. We say good-bye to old friends and hello to new. So retirement is just another step in that natural progression. And it should open as many doors as it closes. In spite of all that is said, with a modicum of good luck (mostly meaning good health) there actually is to be found some solid 18-carat gleam and glitter within the much maligned golden years.

*Why dost thou not retire like a guest sated with the banquet of life, and with calm mind embrace, thou fool, a rest that knows no care?"*

—TITUS LUCRETIUS CARUS,
"De Rerum Natura" (99-55 B.C.)

The first rule of retirement is to avoid the BTFT syndrome (bored to fucking tears). One possibility is to quickly become involved in a major project such as moving, building a house, remodeling or redecorating your present house. Of course these kinds of things cost money, perhaps at a time when you should be carefully watching expenses. But, if you have a few dollars put away, the day after you retire is the time to blow them. Give yourself a needed boost. You can't just retire; you have to launch yourself into retirement. So, take a trip. Join an organization. Buy a dog. Do something to draw a distinct line between your before and after.

*The two foes of human happiness are pain and boredom.*

—ARTHUR SCHOPENHAUER,
*Essays* (1788-1860)

How did I avoid BTFT? Well first thing after retirement I got really sick and then recovered. While I don't recommend this course of action, if that's what I can call it, it did tend to divert my attention. I learned that each day and each night is precious. I now listen to the wind; notice clouds. I ponder the planets and stars. I feel close to nature and I try to avoid cities. During this period (the first year of my retirement) I moved, started building a house, had a granddaughter, took a trip, took another trip, and did a lot of writing, painting and photography. I told my wife, "Money-wise we don't count the first year. But, after that, austerity hovers. We have all these receipts, but no one to send them to. Where's your expense account when you really need it?"

*The more of a somebody you once were, the*
*more difficult it is to revert to being a nobody.*

—ANON.

Retirement is not for everybody. For some the job itself is the fulfillment of all their life's dreams and there can be no other life beyond it. Such people deserve our pity.

*Gone fishin'*

—SIGN ON DOOR

After retirement the days sail by like big silver ships heading for port. The trip is everything. The destination nothing.

> *My foot in the stirrup, my pony won't stand,*
> *Good-bye, Old Paint, I'm a-leavin' Cheyenne.*

—ANON. (COWBOY SONG)

---

## A LETTER NEVER SENT

*Dear Reed:*
*You asked about retirement. It's like I had been in this movie with all these other characters and then the movie ended and while I can replay it over and over in my head, I can't get back in it. I get older and older and the other characters are getting lost one by one and I am finally having to say to myself, "Well I still may be me, but I am sure no longer that guy in the movie." As you know, a couple of years after I retired I went back to visit the old office. It was a little like trying to step back into an hallucination; everything was a bit warped, somehow changed, somehow different. New faces*

*among the old, and even the old ones don't quite look right. And while they are happy to see me for maybe five minutes, after that I can see that what definitely hasn't changed is that the pressures of the jobs are still there and these people are still caught in the trap. They want to be polite, but I am no longer a piece in their puzzle. I have no plans to return again. I don't want to replay that movie anymore. I've moved on. I've got this whole new role I'm working on.*

*Your Friend*

❧

# YOUR LIFE

*Solomon Grundy*
*Born on Monday,*
*Christened on Tuesday,*
*Married on Wednesday,*
*Took ill on Thursday,*
*Worse on Friday,*
*Died on Saturday,*
*Buried on Sunday,*
*And that was the end*
*of Solomon Grundy.*

(Hopefully, the most compelling parts of Mr. Grundy's life story have been omitted.)

By the time we have reached our sixties a nagging question arises, "How have I done? Has my life been meaningful, valuable in any way, productive, successful?" To find answers, we need to dip into the possible meanings of life, because what we are searching for is just how our own singular life might fit into the vast overall puzzle of civilization.

> *Where did you come from, baby dear?*
> *Out of the everywhere, into here.*

—GEORGE MACDONALD,
"At the Back of the North Wind" (1871)

We are *Homo Sapiens*. We have come to visit Earth both collectively and individually from somewhere, or possibly nowhere, and when our visits conclude we go on to somewhere else even if that somewhere also turns out to be nowhere. All of this sounds highly curious and mysterious and raises a myriad of intriguing questions about where we came from, how we should have behaved while here and where our eventual destinations might be. Trying to find answers may prove an impossible task, but the journey will add depth, perception, and probably, consternation to our lives.

> *Life as we find it is too hard for us; it entails too much*
> *pain, too many disappointments, impossible tasks.*
> *We cannot do without palliative remedies.*

—SIGMUND FREUD (1856-1939)

Life has been a maze without a map. Our only guide has

been that of the lives that have gone before us. We had teachers and we had texts. We had, or we did not have, personal objectives. Some of us studied the examples of those who had similar objectives. We tried to follow in the paths of those we admired. We emulated or simulated, or in a very few outstanding cases, surpassed, our idols. Our fondest hopes were to accomplish . . . something meaning-ful. But sadly, at the end, there was no sure way of knowing if we had actually completed anything of worth. Perhaps that is why we are so focused on giving ourselves awards. Here is your Pulitzer Prize, your Nobel Prize, your Emmy, Golden Globe, Oscar, your gold watch; visible, tangible proof of achievement. Of course most of us haven't won awards and have to rely on our own self confidence to get through the week. If we can somehow believe in ourselves, we will find a little peace. It's the next best thing to believ-ing in the existence of Heaven.

> *If I have seen farther, it is by standing*
> *on the shoulders of giants.*
>
> —SIR ISAAC NEWTON (1642-1727)

Human life from its beginning up to the present forms an uninterrupted stream. Like the stars and planets, the human stream is in constant motion made possible not just by procreation, but also by that most amazing human quality of all: our ability to do original work built upon what has been learned and discovered and created by those who lived before our time. Education focuses on absorbing past actions, discoveries and wisdom. All over the world young people study and learn, hoping to build upon the accomplishments of the past. And soon, perhaps, young people will be studying us and learning, and moving along some unsure path made visible by our torches.

> *Life is just a bowl of cherries,*
> *Don't take it serious, life's too mysterious.*
> *You work, you slave, you worry so,*
> *But you can't take your dough when you go, go, go.*
>
> —RAY HENDERSON, LEW BROWN
> ("Life Is Just a Bowl of Chairies," song lyric)

Here is an example of how it goes no matter if the subject is math, cooking, gardening, cosmetology or brain surgery. Say you want to be a stand-up comedian and you want to write your own stuff. Well, first you have to learn all the old jokes because the worst thing that can happen to you is to have someone in the audience say, "Hey, ratface, I already heard dat one." You need new, fresh, original material, not to mention funny. And then you go and try it out at one of the clubs and you either fly or you die. And that's the way it has always been with comedy . . . and space technology, for that matter.

> *That low man seeks a little thing to do,*
> *Sees it and does it;*

> *This high man, with a great thing to pursue,*
> *Dies ere he knows it.*

> —ROBERT BROWNING (1812-89)

Measuring yourself, your life's worth, then becomes a retrospective search to see just where you have fit into the human stream. If you have produced children then the impact of your life will continue. If you have influenced others, if your life has contributed in any way to the times into which you were born, then your life has had impact and you deserve to feel good knowing that however small or large, your life has had meaning that has reached beyond yourself alone. And, there is really no judging how slight or how significant that impact may have been until long beyond your death. Think about Abe Lincoln's mom and dad. They really hadn't a clue.

*Life's but a walking shadow, a poor player*
*That struts and frets his hour upon the stage,*
*And then is heard no more; it is a tale*
*Told by an idiot, full of sound and fury,*
*Signifying nothing.*

—WILLIAM SHAKESPEARE, *Macbeth* (1606)

## A LETTER NEVER SENT

*Dear Charles:*
*The meaning of life; what a topic! It sure was a hot subject*
*way back in our college days when we could play loose and*
*fast with it because there was so much time. And now, pffft,*
*all that time gone and we are still here talking about it, but*
*probably not for long. Let's look each other in the eye, Charlie*
*boy, and admit we don't know, don't have the slightest,*
*slimmest, slip of an idea of what the hell any of it means or if*
*it means anything at all. Where is the wisdom that was to*
*come with age? In archeological terms we humans have not*
*roamed this world long, and yet look at what we have created*
*and look at what we have destroyed. And both the creation*
*and the destruction are accelerating at such an ever increas-*
*ing pace no mathematician could possibly formulate it. The*

*Earth is choking and no one knows the magic Heimlich maneuver to give it breath. I keep thinking about the dinosaurs. I wonder what the meaning of their lives was?*

*Your Friend*

# Forgetfulness

*Pease-Porridge hot, pease-porridge cold,*
*Pease-porridge in the pot, nine days old.*

(Obviously this chef was over sixty and lost track of what he was doing. Now, hopefully, he will also forget about serving it.)

It stands to reason that as you approach the final portion of life your brain becomes overstuffed with education, business acumen, sports stats, the latest IRS regs and trivia, trivia, trivia. There can be room for only so much in a single cranium and when you go to squeeze something additional in, especially something as mundane as where you put the TV remote or exactly how long it has been since you last had sex, other things often get temporarily displaced. Not to worry.

*The horror of that moment,' the King went on,*
*'I shall never forget!'*
*'You will, though,' The Queen said, 'if you*

*don't make a memorandum of it.'*

—LEWIS CARROLL,
*Alice's Adventures In Wonderland* (1832-98)

Here is a joke making the rounds in over-sixty circles: A wife asks her husband to run down to the corner store to get a pint of vanilla ice cream and some chocolate syrup.

"Do you want me to write that down?" she inquires.

"It's only two things," he replies. "Not a problem."

Later he returns and hands her a package containing cheddar cheese.

"I knew you should have written it down," she says. "See here, you forgot the crackers."

*The palest ink is better than the best memory.*

—CHINESE PROVERB

A possible answer to this over-stuffed brain problem is suggested by comedian Steve Martin in a 1998 *New Yorker* magazine article: "One solution for older men is to take all the superfluous data swirling around in the brain and download it into the newly large stomach, where there is plenty of room. This frees the brain to house more relevant information, like the particularly troublesome 'days of the week.'" Not very practical, but at this point most of us would be willing to try anything. We all have to learn to deal with our temporary forgetfulness and there are a number of ways. As the foregoing suggests, we do need to write things down. Then we need to remember to take the list with us and THEN we have to remember to look at the list when it's time for us to know what's on it. Most of us have a strong tendency to believe that we will remember certain facts when we need to. The more probable scenario is that we won't.

*Memory is the thing you forget with.*
—ALEXANDER CHASE, *Perspectives* (1966)

I have long worn glasses for reading and other close-up work. I hate having to take the time to reach into my pocket and put on my glasses, that is if I have remembered to put them in my pocket. This is especially true when it comes to using the touch-tone phone. My eyes are almost good enough to make out the numbers, but not quite. As a result I have to dial a wrong number at least twice before I am convinced I need to put on my specs. I am now in the process of trying to memorize the location of the numbers on the dial pad so I can do it by feel, sort of like touch typing. But since I often have difficulty remembering who it is I am trying to call, this scheme is no doubt doomed to failure.

*Forgetfulness transforms every occurrence into a non-occurrence.*

—Plutarch (AD c.46-c.120)

This same sort of quirky thinking applies to memory loss. At the time your brain first receives new information, you are convinced that you will retain it. ("I will put the package down here, on top of the car. Who could forget that?") But when the moment comes to summon up the necessary information, it is nowhere to be found. We simply get in the car and drive off. We must learn not to trust ourselves. Don't put the package (or the baby) on top of the car; put it on the hood where you can't miss seeing it. Don't put your cocktail glass on the mantel, or in the laundry room, or on the back of the toilet. Put it some place where you'll at least have an even chance of finding it when you suddenly realize it is no longer in your hand. Two reliable spots are the cocktail table or the bar.

*Space, like time, engenders forgetfulness . . .*

—Thomas Mann, *The Magic Mountain* (1924)

Ever leave one room to go to another to do something and when you get there you have no idea why you are there? This is commonplace. No you are probably not getting Alzheimer's. You and your mind are just moving too fast and not paying attention. Don't leave room number one until you fix it in your mind just why you are leaving and where you are going and what you're going to do when you get to room number two. Don't stop to talk with anyone or answer the phone while in transit. And if you do forget, don't worry. This is commonplace . . . or did I mention that already?

> *Better by far that you should forget and smile*
> *Than that you should remember and be sad.*
> —CHRISTINA GEORGIANA ROSSETTI, *Remember* (1862)

How important it is for our favorite NFL team to win the Super Bowl. And, six months later, how impossible it is to even remember which two teams played in it, let alone who won.

> *It's hard to be nostalgic when you can't remember anything.*
> —ANON.

## A LETTER NEVER SENT

*Dear Dan:*

*Sorry I forgot to write. What happened was, I lost your address. Actually, I forgot where I put my address book so I haven't written anybody lately. As a fail-safe, I had also put all addresses on my computer, but I can't remember the command to call them up. I was gonna call your sister to get your address, but her phone number was in the address book. I would have called information, but I can't seem to remember her married name: Molster? Munster? Something like that, but not close enough for information, I suppose. Information is area code plus 555-2211, right? Or is it 1122 ... or 10-10-10 plus something. Never mind, I'll look it up. The phone directory is hopefully too big for me to have misplaced. (Now what was it I was going to write to you about?)*

*Your Uncle*

# MONEY

*A diller, a dollar,*
*A ten o'clock scholar*
(A diller saved, is a diller earned.)

How much money is enough? Elderly people in retirement tend to think about money a lot, and what they often think is that they haven't enough of it. They are concerned that their money will run out before they do. Many of us exaggerate the amount of time we have and underestimate the amount of money we have. We can count the money which makes it a known, but our remaining time is an imponderable. "Plenty of time left," we think, "but will the money last?" Probably.

*It is easier for a camel to go through the eye of a needle,*
*than for a rich man to enter the kingdom of God.*
—*Matthew 19:24*

If we can't take it with us, then, of course no rich man can enter the kingdom of God; the minute he dies he's no longer rich. Death is the great financial equalizer.

> *I'm tired of Love: I'm still more tired of Rhyme.*
> *But Money gives me pleasure all the time.*
>
> —Hilaire Belloc (1870-1953), "Fatigue"

The real global problem is that there is never enough money to go around. Financial security becomes a game of musical chairs. When it comes time to sit down at the dinner table there are always fewer places than hungry people. So, earning a living evolves as a very competitive game not just for the wealthy but for everybody who wants to stay on the north side of the poverty line. For those of us no longer in the rat race it is not all that different. We do have some help in the form of Social Security, Medicare and reduced prices at the movies, travel and National Parks. We no longer have to "keep up with the Jones's" (though we really didn't have to in the first place). We can wear old, comfy clothes, drive vehicles nearly as ancient as ourselves, and get a double mortgage on the homestead for the kids to worry about later. We do still have to eat, however, and a beer with lunch tastes pretty good.

*Money is better than poverty, if only for financial reasons.*

—WOODY ALLEN, *Without Feathers* (1972)

In the jungle, there is no need for money. The food and balance is provided by nature. In the rest of the world money is the substitute for the tooth and claw, the water hole and the banana tree. And at times it works even better than the paw-to-mouth method if only because we seldom actually have to eat one another. Old toothless lionesses no longer able to hunt, starve to death. Humans are able to predict and thus provide for their old age, and starving, in this country at least, is rare.

> *I don't know much about being a millionaire,*
> *but I'll bet I'd be darling at it.*

—DOROTHY PARKER ((1893-1967)

For those of us with not quite enough money—those whose out-go always seems just a tad higher than the income—all hope is not lost. There is the lottery. No one we know ever wins the lottery (here I'm talking the seven-plus-figure prizes) but we believe that someone wins and no matter what the odds, that some one might as well be us. And, if it did happen that this time it turned out to be us looking google-eyed at the winning numbers and matching them over and over to our stub (once we located our stub, whew! ) and it kept checking out and we actually were the winner, WE would certainly know what best to do with all that loot. WE wouldn't be so stupid to blow it on a new Rolls and an ocean-front villa. WE would be generous and give a bunch to The Salvation Army and to friends and family members suddenly less well off than ourselves. (And if you, my friend, happen to win we hope that you will feel exactly the same way toward us.)

*Why is there so much month left at the end of the money?*

—ANON.

If we are unable to increase our income, then it's a very good idea to take a look at our spending habits and see if there isn't some way we can stretch the money we have. First we rule out all those insidious things we have to pay such as federal, state, county and local taxes, rent (or mortgage or real estate taxes), insurance (car, house, health, belongings), garbage pickup, cable or dish TV fees, heating oil or gas, electric, phone, cell phone, water, car registration and driver's license (not to mention the car itself), personal property taxes, safe deposit box, maintenance on car and house, clothing and, if anything is left over, food. All the remaining money we can spend on fun stuff like the dentist and speculating in the stock market. All it takes is a little belt tightening, right?

> *I haven't heard of anybody who wants to stop living*
> *because of the cost.*

—FRANK MCKINLEY "KIN" HUBBARD (1868-1930)

## A LETTER NEVER SENT

*Dear J. D.:*

*Just because you do my taxes for me doesn't mean you are to blame for the fact that I have to pay taxes. I constantly try to keep that in mind, but it does seem a bit unfair of you, when I have gone to so much trouble throughout the year to keep things under tight control, when, annually, about the middle of March, you let me know that my tax forms are ready and must be signed and sent, when you damn well know that it's not the signing or the postage that I am concerned about. What I want to know, and what you know I want to know, is what's it gonna cost me? I know that you'll say that sometimes I get something back, but I seriously doubt that ever actually happened and if it did you just turned it around and* gave it right back to them as my next quarterly payment. If I can't spend what I get back then, in my estimation, I didn't get it back. I have been paying quarterly (right?) just like you told me to. And, look here, at the stubs of my pension checks, those monthly deductions are federal taxes. So why, now, at the end of everything do I owe more? Sorry, there I go again. The IRS, that branch of government so evil that even those in other branches of government detest it, must be the cause. Certainly not you, J. D., I'm sure. You are just the messenger, and we mustn't kill the messenger. But, I've always wondered, J. D., when April 15 rolls around, do you owe them or do they owe you?

*Your Friend*

# LONELINESS

*There was a crooked man, and he walked a crooked mile,*
*He found a crooked sixpence against a crooked style;*
*He bought a crooked cat, which caught a crooked mouse,*
*And they all lived together in a little crooked house.*

(When a person is too much alone, he or she is apt to behave somewhat pecurlarly, but hopefully not crookedly.)

A
s we age our world shrinks and our friends and acquaintances diminish. Retirement often means moving to a new location and making new friends can be a chore. Even for those who stay put, many of their old friends move away; some become sick or even die. Family members, too, move away and a once large circle closes in. It is not a pleasant scenario, especially for gregarious people who have been used to an active social whirl. Getting older may not be easy, but there may be solutions to these problems for those who maintain a positive attitude. Keeping the mind active and focused on projects of personal interest

really works. Whether it's cooking, sewing, crosswords, fishing, a new pet, movies, golf, bridge, bingo or other activities that will bring us in contact with people who have similar problems and desires, mental and/or physical activity in a social setting can go a long way toward an improved outlook on life.

*No one would choose a friendless existence on condition of having all the other things in the world.*

—ARISTOTLE, *Nicomachean Ethics* (4th c. B.C.)

For some, loneliness may produce a longing so severe that even death can seem a welcome alternative. And yet others actually seem to prefer being alone. In reality, it only takes one other person to cure you of your loneliness, though, conversely, it may only take one other person to make you wish for solitude. Choose new friends with care.

*One may have a blazing hearth in one's soul,
yet no one ever comes to sit by it.*

—VINCENT VAN GOGH letters (1853-98)

By the time you have reached your sixties you have earned a rich personal heritage. You have been places, seen things, had experiences that call out to be shared with others.

Socializing with persons in your own age group will bring out all the many things you have in common. The music, humor and history we share with our contemporaries makes us members of the same club. This camaraderie can be a basis for forming new friendships that can be as strong as any you have ever had.

> *My heart is a lonely hunter that hunts on a lonely hill.*
> —WILLIAM SHARP (1855-1905)

The three degrees of loneliness are: alone for an hour, alone for a day and alone forever. When the one dearest to our heart has gone there is no solace. Time becomes our only friend, but time has never moved at a slower pace. We have to try to outlive our loneliness. One way may be to face it head on by writing your own personal history for your children and grandchildren, though mostly just for yourself. This will not only give you an opportunity to reexamine your life, but to discover new personal insights that may help you better cope with being alone.

> *The biggest disease today is not leprosy or tuberculosis,*
> *but rather the feeling of being unwanted.*
> —MOTHER THERESA (1910-97)

It's wonderful to be alone in your room when you know somebody else is at home with you; but it's dreadful to be alone there when all the other rooms are empty. Without friends the world can become a very hostile place, if you let it. Alive or dead, it can seem that no one cares about your existence. If this is the way you feel, then now is the time you absolutely must seek help from anyone you know: your doctor, lawyer, church, neighbor. If this fails, get out the yellow pages and look up "Crises Intervention" or "Social Service Organizations." Look for listings about "seniors" or "adults." Help is waiting out there for you, but it is up to you to make the first call.

*Lonely people talking to each other can make each other lonelier.*
—LILLIAN HELLMAN "The Autumn Garden" (1951)

## A LETTER NEVER SENT

*Dear Gladys:*

*I saw a picture of you the other day and you were very young and lovely. I never saw you that young, but then, you never saw me this old. And what would you think of me if we could walk hand in hand and I could show you this and that. What would you think of this old fellow who says you should know him well? We have been apart for 46 years, almost as many years as you lived, and I have missed you all that time. But, have you missed me? That is the question; have you missed me? If I knew the answer to that, then I would know all the answers.*

*Your Loving Son*

# FRIENDSHIP

*Rub-a-dub-dub,*
*Three men in a tub,*
*And who do you think they be?*
*The butcher, the baker,*
*The candlestick-maker,*
*And all of them went to sea!*

(These three old pals were reportedly on good terms when they left the dock, but by the time they returned, who knows? A sea voyage, especially one in a tub, can stress even the closest of friendships.)

Friendship, unlike marriage, requires no legal document. The distinctions between acquaintance, good friend, best friend, true friend, new friend, old friend, fair-weather friend, a friend of a friend and a friend in need are subject to individual, not legal, interpretation and will mean different things to different people. There are friends you hold in high regard, and others you merely tolerate. There are those who are your friends because of themselves, and others who remain your friends in spite of themselves. There are some things that only a friend can do for you. For example, only a friend can betray you.

> *Foresake not an old friend; for the new is not*
> *comparable to him: a new friend is as a new wine;*
> *when it is old, thou shall drink it with pleasure.*
>
> —*The Apocrypha* (c. 300 B.C.—100 A.D.)

The very young only have new friends, but by the time you have reached sixty you will have old as well as new friends. Some old friends you may not have seen for forty years or more, but in your mind they exist as friends, and if the phone rings and a voice asks, "Do you remember me," you will say "Yes, of course I do," and go on from there. And if you meet one of these old friends at a reunion or just by chance and you begin together to recall old deeds and misdeeds, you will both say, "Well it seems just like yesterday," and "Isn't it amazing how we can take up just where we left off," and "It's been forty years you say? Forty years? No. No way." And you will enjoy a wonderful re-connection and shake hands or hug and say good-bye, probably forever, because neither of you will have another forty years.

*If we have no friends we have no pleasure,*
*and if we have them we are sure to lose them*
*and be doubly pained by the loss.*

—Abraham Lincoln (1850's)

Eventually, either you lose your friends or your friends lose you. That's why people in their sixties and older read the obits. Over so many years through school and business, marriage and socializing, we collect a good many acquaintances and we like to keep track. We have address books and perhaps Christmas card lists but even so, some names get misplaced over time and that means that the people are misplaced in our minds and we can't seem to recapture them. Without friends and family we are alone in the world, so each person we lose or misplace diminishes us and we can sense the edge of anxiety as our list constantly dwindles. New friends and family members are important, but they can in no way replace the old ones. Friends of our own generation are a reflection of ourselves and as each one vanishes, our own image is dimmed to that degree.

*We shall never have friends, if we expect*
*to find them without fault.*

—Thomas Fuller, M.D. (*Gnomologia* 1732)

Terminating a friendship is both difficult and painful. Why would anybody want to lose a friend on purpose? Let me list the ways: money, trust, boredom. The big three. It is the unwritten rule of friendship that dollar loans are not offered or taken and expenses on trips or out-to-eat should be split evenly. The whole purpose of a close friendship is to have someone you can trust and confide in. If the confidence is violated—end of friendship. And, finally, people change over time, interests evolve, all of us eventually become different people. It is inevitable that some friendships will not survive. This is what makes enduring friendships so valuable; they have continued in spite of all the problems. Two people who like each other have taken the trouble to keep the lines open over time and space and have avoided all the pitfalls along the way.

> *You cannot be friends upon any other terms than upon the terms of equality.*
>
> —WOODROW WILSON (speech made in 1913)

If an old friend gets in financial trouble and you have the means, your tendency is to help your friend out with a gift. Or, if over the years you have been financially successful and your friend has not been so fortunate, you might wish to invite him or her to join you on a trip all expenses paid (by you). Such situations and actions do not always destroy the friendship, but they do always put such a strain on the relationship that it will never again be what it once was. One party may expect gratitude, or feel exploited, while the other may feel diminished having been demoted to junior partner in the relationship.

> *It's Friendship, Friendship,*
> *Just a perfect blendship,*
> *When other friendships have been forgot,*
> *Ours will still be hot!*
>
> —COLE PORTER (song lyric 1939)

## A Letter Never Sent

*Dear Betty:*

*While I haven't seen you in more than fifteen years (can't believe it) ours is my oldest active friendship; active to the extent that we exchange Christmas messages and the occasional phone call. I guess one way to keep from putting any stress on a friendship is to keep it one ice, like ours. After the Los Angeles quake we temporarily lost contact and I made* some calls but couldn't find you and so I considered the worst possibility, and then I couldn't get the thought out of my head. I was deeply upset, but then came your Christmas card and we were back in touch. I remember I was five years old when you moved next door and we had the opportunity to grow up together. Our bedrooms faced each other's across the driveway and we had a lot of window communication. We even had those paper-cup-and-string phones which, at the time, we thought worked pretty good. And our summers in Long Island were idyllic, so much so that you still keep the house there. And you always ask us to visit. And we always want to, but haven't made it yet. We are both more used to having company than being company. But time is slipping and sliding away. How many others do we know who intimately knew our parents, our childhoods? We shared so much, Betty, we must find the time to share just a little more.

*Your Old Friend*

# HEALTH AND SICKNESS

*Jack and Jill went up the hill*
*To fetch a pail of water;*
*Jack fell down and broke his crown,*
*And Jill came tumbling after.*

(It is a little known fact that both Jack and Jill were in their
mid-sixties and qualified for Medicare.)

O n some days we feel as if we could live forever, but
a casual glance at our reflection brings us to reality.
The face is lined and loose around the skull. The
color is gone from the ever-thinning hair. The stomach pro-
trudes and the chest or breasts sag. The legs are more
spindly, the upper arms slack-to-sloppy. Even those among
us who are dedicated exercise nuts can see that despite all
efforts, our exteriors are deteriorating. We can't help but
imagine, if this is what is taking place outside, the horrors
that must be happening inside.

*Although the world is full of suffering,*
*it is full also of the overcoming of it.*

—HELEN KELLER (1880-1968)

There is a machine that can tell the truth from a lie, another that can measure the power of an earthquake half way round the world and still another that can tell us how old the most ancient piece of rock or bone is. But there is no machine that can measure pain. Is my headache worse that your backache? Is she really suffering or is she faking? Is his pain debilitating, or can he work his way through it? Pain is judged inside a person's head; that is the only meaningful measurement. There is no device that can tell you if a certain pain is worse than death. That you have to decide for yourself.

*It's wonderful being an old man. . . .*
*I feel better at 61 than I did at 51, or 41.*

—KRIS KRISTOFFERSON, *Parade* 1998

We should always keep in mind that good health is a temporary condition to be savored when experienced, like good weather.

*The very first requirement in a hospital is that it
should do the sick no harm.*

—Florence Nightingale (1820-1910)

There are two kinds of illnesses: those that you may recover from and those that you cannot. Believing that you will get better helps you through the first kind. Fear that you will be sick for the rest of your life presents an added psychological burden for the second. But here is something to consider if you believe you are permanently ill. New treatments are being discovered every day, and it is now possible to live a fairly normal life with many incurable diseases (diabetes, Grave's disease, lupus, even many forms of cancer). So it is best to keep the most optimistic outlook possible, for while there is life there is hope—hope that new treatments will become available; that your terminal diagnosis was in error; that a new physician will bring a different perspective and a brighter prognosis; that for whatever reason, remission will take place; and there will be additional life to live and enjoy.

*Medicine being a compendium of the successive and contradictory mistakes of practitioners, when we summon the wisest of them to our aid, the chances are that we*

*may be relying on a scientific truth the error of which will*
*be recognized in a few years' time.*

—MARCEL PROUST, *Remembrance of Things Past* (1913-27)

In my own case I was misdiagnosed and told by the specialist I had but two years to live; then cut wide open for, what turned out to be, a search in vain for some evidence to support his conclusions. Of course if I had not survived I would not be here now to complain about it, so I am not entirely bitter. My ugly, still painful (after four years) scar serves me as a reminder to be thankful and to enjoy and make good use of my time. My thanks here is to that "second opinion" doctor who told me I would be putting in some more time on Earth; enough time to discover what the actual cause of my eventual death might be.

> *Early to rise and early to bed makes a male*
> *healthy, wealthy and dead.*
>
> —JAMES THURBER, *Fables For Our Time* (1940)

If you are a fighter, life is a battle to the end. We are all too well aware of the eventual conclusion, but many of us prefer to fight the good fight anyway. We jog, walk, lift and stretch. We select our foods with care. We watch our weight. We get regular medical check ups. Yet there are many among us who do not choose to go this route. I believe that the latter group is less content, less happy. It seems to me that we should always participate as much as possible in life instead of just letting life run out. It's true we all end up the same, but while we are here we should never give up.

> . . . in sickness and in health, to love and to cherish,
> till death us do part.

> —Marriage vows, *The Book of Common Prayer* (1928)

---

## A LETTER NEVER SENT

*Dear Jim:*

*I guess near the top of any list of awful things is being sick. I have been sick enough in my life, from early childhood on, possibly because both of my parents were smokers; later perhaps because I was a smoker, a habit, as you know, both Anne and I have kicked. After my serious illness four years ago, I felt that I had earned some kind of glory points that would bring good things to my life and keep me well, for a while anyway. Actually, though, the glory points should go to those who unselfishly, without complaint, live with and care for the sick. You have many such points, my friend. Mary, too. And Anne, though since I recovered some time ago, she may have used up most of hers by now. We fervently hope we do not have to earn more any time soon. We have too many married friends who are one well and one sick. The one who is well is almost as constrained and confined as the one who is ill. In those marriages the "for better" of the wedding vows has slipped by, and the "for worse" has become a stark reality. But, because of the amazing power of love, these unions grow even stronger. In the end, love prevails even when one of the partners cannot.*

*Your Friend*

꧁꧂

# HAIR STYLES

*He promised to bring me a bunch of blue ribbons,*
*To tie up my bonnie brown hair.*

(Rumor has it that Johnny was so long at the fair, her bonnie brown hair had long ago turned gray by the time he returned.)

Many people, especially women, color their hair as soon as the first indication of gray appears. They color it regularly at home or at the beauty parlor as the years continue to slip by. At some point in time, certainly by sixty years of age, their blond or brown or red tresses no longer mesh easily with their creased faces, even those visages that have been stretched to the max by cosmetic surgery. Perhaps the time has come for reassessment and the decision to release one's true hair color from its time warp so that it can rejoin the rest of the body. Most of us will silently thank those we must look at regularly for this intelligent choice.

*How ill white hairs become a fool and jester!*
—WILLIAM SHAKESPEARE, *The Life Of King Henry V* (1599)

A man can say a lot with his hair—unless he's bald. Then what he's saying may be subject to misinterpretation. Of course he can always continue to make a statement by wearing a hairpiece. Unfortunately, that statement usually is: "Hey look. I'm wearing a hairpiece."

*Regrets are the natural property of grey hairs.*
—CHARLES DICKENS, *Martin Chuzzlewit* (1844)

When you are young, you are free to speak with your hairstyle. When you are old, your hairstyle too often speaks without your consent. Today, however, there are prescription medications to deal with male hair loss that really can make a difference. As they say, ask your doctor.

*Darling I am growing old,*
*Silver threads among the gold*
—E. E. ROXFORD, song lyric (1873)

White hair is the crown we all have earned (except Ronald Reagan and a few other suspects). Wear it proudly.

*It is not white hair that engenders wisdom.*

—MENANDER (c.342-292 B.C.)

Why is it that young women wear their hair in a variety of styles, but women over sixty-five tend to look as if they all belong to the same white-cotton-candy-hair club.

*Hair today; gone tomorrow.*

—ANON.

(It seems no one wanted to take credit for this one.)

Men have only one hair advantage over women. What they lose from their scalps, they can replace on their chins.

*But the very hairs of your head are all numbered.*

—*Matthew 0:29 - 30*

## A Letter Never Sent

*Dear Ruel:*

*Except in photos, I never saw you with hair. You lost most of it before I was born. And yet I never thought of you as bald; it was just your natural look and I loved it with all my heart. You were a distinguished looking man. A man admired and respected by all. Hair had nothing to do with it. And as I grew up it never occurred to me to do anything special with my hair. I grew it short for sports, longer for girls. I kept expecting to go bald because you had gone bald. I hoped I could put it off until my wedding day. And now that I am years older than you were when you died at sixty-six, I still have just enough left to comb. If hair were of any importance, that would be quite some accomplishment.*

*Your Loving Son*

❧

# FEARS AND PHOBIAS

*Ladybug, ladybug, fly away home,*
*Your house is on fire, and your children will burn.*

(Or maybe it's just your overactive imagination.)

Ernest Hemingway defined courage as "grace under pressure." He was a brave man and took many risks during his lifetime that required considerable daring. He was wounded in war, and he was injured many times during his hyper-active life. All of this he survived with good humor. But when the time came for him to face the infirmities of old age, his manic-depressive personality (and ill-conceived shock treatments) twisted his mind and he could see only the downside. At the age of sixty-two he blew his brains out. Old age can bring more pressure than grace.

*Cowards die many times before their deaths;*
*The valiant never taste of death but once.*

—WILLIAM SHAKESPEARE, *Julius Caesar* (1598-1600)

Until put to the test, most of us can't help wondering how we might react in dangerous situations. All of us are potential cowards (as well as heroes) and it is possible to have lived a long and sheltered life and not yet discovered for sure just what we are made of. Now is our chance.

> *Canst thou not minister to a mind diseas'd,*
> *Pluck from the memory a rooted sorrow,*
> *Raze out the written troubles of the brain,*
> *And with some sweet oblivious antidote*
> *Cleanse the stuff'd bosom of that perilous stuff*
> *Which weighs upon the heart.*
>
> —WILLIAM SHAKESPEARE, *MacBeth* (1606)

The dark corners of your mind are darker than any back alley and can be dangerous to your mental health. There are a bunch of buttons and switches in our heads and when the wrong ones get pushed, trouble in its most devious form may result. Like dreams and nightmares with their inside-out, upside-down, illogical shapes and stories, the mind in its wakeful state can also produce anxiety, depression and other unwelcome and unfamiliar effects. A sunny day or a good feeling can instantly be turned about and the half-full glass become half empty.

*Where no hope is left, is left no fear.*

—JOHN MILTON (1608-74)

Fear comes in multitudinous forms but basically breaks down into two categories: fear of the known and fear of the unknown. It is the second one that is the scariest.

*I will show you fear in a handful of dust.*

—T. S. ELLIOT "The Waste Land" 1922

Fear dwells within us all. The ability to keep it under control is what reveals the inner stuff. Facing our own mortality, year after year, as well as that of our most dearly loved ones, is seriously trying and can produce crippling anxiety. Looking on the dark side or looking on the bright side is the choice. Trying to consciously make it is the difficulty.

*Who's afraid of the Big Bad Wolf,*
*The Big Bad Wolf, the Big Bad Wolf?*

—Frank Churchill/Ann Ronell, *Three Little Pigs* (1933)

"The only thing we have to fear is fear itself." Of course Franklin Roosevelt was speaking in 1933 when bank closings were a national problem. Nevertheless it was a profound and eloquent sentence and it remains one of his most famous lines. Knowing, however, that we are only afraid of our fears, doesn't really help the truly anxious. They can be afraid of being afraid of being afraid. The only thing they have to fear is the fear of fear.

*Fear tastes like a rusty knife and do not let her into your house.*
—JOHN CHEEVER, *The Wapshot Chronicle* (1957)

## A LETTER NEVER SENT

*Dear Z:*

*In latter years our minds may dwell too much on our approaching demises. Quick and unexpected? Protracted and painful? To entertain no fearful thoughts concerning this would be unnatural. To let such concerns severely diminish our remaining days would be a tragic waste. Very often the state of mind we have is the state of mind we seek. The world out-side our rooms is much the same as it was when we owned it. Clouds still scud in skies reflecting each dusk and dawn. We should not miss a sunset. The air stirs and great fish still swim the oceans. Trees give sound to the wind and animals still dwell in the forests. Young and beautiful people are still young and beautiful, and to see them frolicking on the beaches today is to know there is a future; that life goes on. We must* struggle to put future-fear aside and fight the bloody battles to make each remaining day the best that it can be. If we can concentrate on the fight, our fears will be set aside and at special moments our eyes can make us young.

*Your Friend*

# HAPPINESS

*Old King Cole was a merry old soul,*
*And a merry old soul was he;*
*He called for his pipe,*
*and he called for his bowl,*
*And he called for his fiddlers three.*

(It doesn't necessarily take three fiddlers, a pipe and a bowl—
of what?—to be a merry old soul, but it couldn't hurt.)

Some days you just wake up that way and climb out on the right side and stay there all day. What combination of physical and mental factors bring on this unexpected euphoria? Who knows? Take notes. Be aware. Be sure it's not just the Prozac.

> *. . . Life, Liberty and the Pursuit of Happiness.*
>
> —THOMAS JEFFERSON,
> *Declaration of Independence* (1776)

Happiness is a temporary, euphoric state much sought after by most everybody. But, as so many discover to their dismay, an "unalienable" right to pursue happiness is no guarantee of good results. I don't know who it was who tagged the retirement years as "golden." It had to have been some poor hard working slob who hadn't had a two-week vacation in years. From that perspective retirement would surely appear bright, shiny and precious. But reality seldom matches expectations. There is nothing inherently bad about the combination of a regular pension and/or Social Security check and no time clock to punch; in fact, there is a lot to be said for it. But there is more to happiness than just money and leisure, leisure and money. A feeling of worth, of being needed, being loved, being well, are all necessary ingredients to a well-adjusted, if not blissful, mind and soul.

*Happiness makes up in height what it lacks in length.*

—ROBERT FROST (1874-1963)

Unhappiness (or happiness) is not a constant state; it ebbs and flows, comes and goes. However, as it might say on the label of a bottle of medicine, if your unhappy state persists for more than a month, see your doctor (keeping in mind that it will certainly take at least another month to get the appointment). If you are enjoying a prolonged happy state of mind and it continues for weeks on end, you may be nuts, but I would advise you to simply leave it alone and enjoy it. Whatever you do, don't try to analyze it. Trying to comprehend what happiness consists of can only lead to depression.

> . . . where happiness fails, existence remains a
> mad and lamentable experiment.
>
> —GEORGE SANTAYANA,
> *The Life of Reason* (1905-06)

Happy people don't jump off tall buildings or asphyxiate themselves in their garages. One may be content at the very end of life without being ecstatic. Many of us in our advanced state are still able to derive a great deal of pleasure just from being alive. We face reality, but we just do not care to dwell on it. We were appraised of the rules of life and death early on. We accepted them when we were young and we accept them now. Nothing has changed except our location on the longevity scale. We know that the alternative to happiness is unhappiness. As long as we are able to, we choose the former.

*We are happier in many ways when we are old*
*than when we were young. The young sow*
*wild oats. The old grow sage.*

—SIR WINSTON CHURCHILL (1874-1965)

Upon reaching the age of sixty-five I felt a certain relief. The strain of competition seemed to vanish, and was to be replaced with a feeling of unfettered freedom to pursue my own desires. Not that I lost all ambition. I still wanted to achieve, but I wanted to be the judge of my own work, the sole creator and decision maker. And if my efforts were successful in some critical or financial way then I could (modestly) accept credit and toast myself in front of the mirror with an extra ounce and a half of Famous Grouse. Or, if my efforts flunked those outside tests, I could chastise myself (gently) and console myself, perhaps not in the mirror, but still with an extra ounce and a half of Famous Grouse. At my age the work itself is its own reward; success comes with merely doing. (Famous Grouse is also its own reward.)

*Happy days are here again,*
*The skies above are clear again:*
*Let us sing a song of cheer again,*
*Happy days are here again!*

—JACK YELLEN, song lyric (1929)

While happiness takes many forms and is expressed in many ways from a baby's gurgle to a lover's groan, it is absolutely necessary to life. The most telling, individual point of inquiry is, what is it that makes us happy? A professional hit man may find deep satisfaction in a job well done, but it is a blatant form of selfish joy. If our happiness hurts others, how valuable can it be? Age takes much of the selfishness out of being happy (there are very few hit men over sixty). It is a time of life when, if our lottery ticket turns out to be a winner, we feel more joy for our young family members than we do for ourselves. We know there is a changing of the guard and that our happiness depends on their happiness.

> *Happy trails to you until we meet again.*
>
> —DALE EVANS, song lyric (1951)

## A LETTER NEVER SENT

*Dear Alice:*
*Now it's as if we have swapped places. You had the money, I had none. You took obvious pleasure in lending me a helping hand. You were an old woman left alone. Husband, brother,*

parents all gone. And, no children. Whenever I needed the help, you were there with an open purse. So happy to be generous. Even though you have been gone now for sixty years I can hear your rich laughter and see your smile. I can still feel your love for me and mine for you. The main difference is that now I understand you. When I was young and needy I used to think I had to con you into giving me the dollars I thought I needed to buy this or that. Now I know you did it because it gave you pleasure, just as it gives me pleasure to give to my own daughter and granddaughter. Of course you didn't have to be generous and understanding and loving. But you found your happiness in my happiness just as I now find mine in theirs. Your happiness lives on in me and I am passing it on.

*Your Loving Nephew*

# Sex after Sixty

*There was an old woman who lived in a shoe,*
*She had so many children she didn't know what to do.*

(This should read, "She had so many children
she didn't know what not to do.")

I f you don't believe that there is sex after sixty, even seventy and eighty, just read the medical books. They will tell you that, yes, there is; perhaps a tiny bit less often, a smidgen less hot, but it will be there for both of you, all of us, forever, so to speak. Unfortunately, these books were written by people in their thirties and forties fantasizing about their own futures.

*When a man tells me he's run out of steam in the sex*
*department, I'll tell him, 'Count your blessings; you've*
*escaped from the clutches of a cruel tyrant. Enjoy!'*

—RICHARD J. NEEDHAM

In the beginning of a close relationship, sex is about organs and glands and positions and where to put what because in the early going, love is all about sex. Much later on, sex is all about love.

*There is many a good tune played on an old fiddle.*

—ANON.

With the advent of the pill that promises erections till the end of time, it seems the song writers may have been right all along: the secret of true love is the right chemistry. And this pill can make the chemistry right even when it's wrong. But, though Viagra does indeed work, the picture may not really be quite so rosy as the general public has been led to believe. A great deal depends on the general health of both the partners, and poor general health in later life is all too common. It only takes one ill partner to halt marital sexual intercourse, pill or no pill.

*Is Sex Necessary?*

—E. B. WHITE/JAMES THURBER, book title (1929)

Is over-the-hill impotence a medical problem that really needed solving? Should insurance companies pay for Viagra and other prescriptions designed to cure impotence by age? No question that sex is the primary human distraction. The phrase, "It's better than sex," really means nothing is better, at least nothing brings such immediate gratification, such powerful physical satisfaction. No one over sixty wants to quit eating. Food is good. So is a cool drink on a beautiful day with trees rustling in a light wind. So is sex. Bottom line: We all want to live as complete beings for as long as possible. A continuing sex life is one of the human components that makes us complete.

> *When I was 19, I desired 19-year-old women.*
> *Now that I am 95, I still desire 19-year-old women.*
>
> —attributed to GEORGE BURNS (1896-1996)

In marriages that have lasted forty or more years the partners have not only grown used to one another, they have grown old together. Some people are able to deal with this situation with a combination of love, pride and devotion. Others see it as a developing nightmare. Can lovers who fell for one another in their early twenties when they were vigorous, youthful and sexy, remain lovers in their sixties, seventies or beyond when so much has changed? Answer is, some can, some can't. For those who can, the rewards are considerable and when the inevitable happens and death forces separation upon them, the surviving partner will find much solace in the knowledge that their union endured, overcame, persevered to the end. Those who break up and take up with new, younger partners may enjoy a brief euphoric interlude, but are still left to face the eventual limits of their own mortality.

*Use it or loose it.*

—Anon.

The doctor carefully explained erection options to his impotent heart patient who could not take Viagra. There could be surgery to insert either an inflatable or a semi-stiff device into his penis, both promising to make intercourse possible without a normal erection. He could give himself an injection if his fear of needles didn't exceed his desire for intercourse. Or, he could insert a tiny capsule a inch or so into his penis to work its wonders but with probable side effects similar to a sharp kick in the groin. But the cure the doctor most highly recommended was a $400-plus plastic pump. The male inserts his penis into a tube and he or his partner pumps to create a vacuum which should cause an erection. A ring is then placed around the base of the hopefully now stiff penis and the contraption is removed. This really works, the doctor will assure him, handing over a quite graphic color brochure. But what the doctor will probably not tell the man is that by simply rolling on an ordinary, everyday condom he can likely get the same results at a very low cost.

*Is it not strange that desire should so many years outlive performance?*

—WILLIAM SHAKESPEARE,
*King Henry IV Part II* (1598)

One of the most wonderful things about latter life love making is that foreplay can last up to a month. "Speedy" Gonzalos must have been a young man because there's is no such thing as a quickie past the age of seventy.

*Lover, Come Back To Me*

—OSCAR HAMMERSTEIN II, song title (1928)

Love doesn't end with sex. Love is more enduring than sex. Love is purer than sex. When it's going right, sex is the bonus part of love. When it's over, sex is the shared memory that makes love continue to be special. While sexual intercourse may cease, sex itself lingers in the mind and body so that lovers remain lovers until the end.

*Amoebas at the start*
*Were not complex;*
*They tore themselves apart*
*And started sex.*

—Arthur Guiterman (1871-1943)

---

## A Letter Never Sent

*Dear Jack:*
*Sex is the ultimate distraction. Perhaps we should all be rendered eunuchs at forty. Fifteen years of copulation, breeding, fornication, buggery, rape, child molestation, whoring around, singles bars, gay bars, cross dressing and other embarrassments seems more than ample. At forty our vision would clear and we could proceed with making the world a better place. Instead we stumble on—forty, fifty, sixty, seventy, and we are still at it, doing the same old thing only doing it worse. Like our tennis and golf games, we keep swinging away in some desperate attempt to remain who we used to be. The clear fact it seems, is that humans are compelled to have sex in one form or another until circumstances force an end. And yet, a sexual relationship between loving, faithful partners of forty or more years can be acutely beautiful, even spiritual in nature. The touching of the bodies, whether the act is fully consummated*

*or not, nurtures and deepens the relationship. Toward the end, fond memories of past occurrences waft through our minds and we know that because of our love and sex we have reproduced all that is most precious to us. We know that our bloodline will continue and this somehow softens the impact of our inevitable demise.*

*Your Friend*

# Wisdom

*There was a man in our town,*
*And he was wondrous wise;*
*He jumped into a bramble bush*
*And scratched out both his eyes.*

(I don't make these up. I suppose, like many men who are assumed to possess great wisdom, this man was quite elderly and his mind was, well, wandering. He probably thought he was jumping into a bubble bath with a young Elizabeth Taylor.)

The wise old owl knew. What? Everything. He had wisdom which made him an oracle, which made him speak as a god. Legend has it that wise and old go hand in hand. Live long enough and you attain wisdom, a depth and breadth of knowledge worthy of young disciples. Unfortunately, unlike owls, human wisdom has its limits. While living long may teach about life and living, it can offer no special insights into other spheres. The 100-year-old man or woman still has to face an uncertain tomorrow, same as the rest of us.

*Not by age but by capacity is wisdom acquired.*

—TITUS MACCIUS PLAUTUS (254-184 B.C.)

We have all known men and women we considered to be wise, or at least wiser than most. Many of us believe that our mothers and/or fathers were wise. Whether they were wise or just seemed that way is moot. When we were growing up, they were wise in comparison to ourselves. If they were good parents, they tried to point us in the right direction and they were selfless and genuinely considered our own welfare ahead of their own. Easy to see, as selfish little brats, why we considered them so wise. And then we became the parents and we were doing what we could for our own broods and if we seemed wise to them, we certainly did not seem wise to ourselves. Like beauty, wisdom seems to exist in the eyes of the beholders.

> *I've studied now Philosophy*
> *And Jurisprudence, Medicine—*
> *And even, alas! Theology—*
> *From end to end with labor keen;*
> *And here, poor fool! with all my lore*
> *I stand, no wiser than before.*

—JOHANN WOLFGANG VON GOETHE, *Faust* (1808)

People on the evening news, local and national, have a warped perception of what the viewing public wants, I believe. At least twice a month they will do a story that has something to do with birds and tell us, giggling back and forth if there are two of them, "Now, here's one for the birds (chuckle, chuckle)." I seriously doubt they could do a story about a bird without prefacing it that way. They must be taught to do that in journalism school. "This one's for the birds! He-he-he-he." Or, how about Ground Hog Day. Every journalist knows that the public is simply dying to find out if the little beast saw its shadow. Actually, no one in his right mind cares a whit, and yet they persist. The list goes on and on and I realize that I digress, so I will try to return to my original point, to wit, every time the news people can find some poor chap who has lived for one hundred years, they descend upon him or her and ask, "To what do you owe your extended life span? What can you tell our huge audience that will help them reach one hundred." And the poor subject of all this unwanted attention gazes somewhat vacantly in the direction of the camera, and mumbles a reply like, "I always put honey on both sides of my toast," or "Every Thursday night I sleep with a litchi nut under my pillow" or some other curious piece of mind-blowing wisdom. So if you wish to attain wisdom, don't wait until you are one hundred, because to be wizened is not necessarily to be wise.

> *Four be the things I am wiser to know:*
> *Idleness, sorrow, a friend, and a foe.*
> —DOROTHY PARKER, *Enough Rope* (1927)

Having said all the above I decided to briefly interview a family friend who was 97 years old (at the time we talked) to test my theories and her wisdom. We call her Mama B. and she quilts as well as drives her own car. She lives alone (she has been a widow since 1971 and "doesn't want somebody around all the time") in her house in northern Louisiana and she seemed quite willing and interested in letting me ask her a few questions. First I inquired, "Do you know more today than you did when you were younger?" And she told me, "Yes, because I didn't know much when I was young." Oookay. "Well then, Mama B., what do you know?" She didn't hesitate, "Keeping house. Working. Stay busy or go crazy." Next, I thought, I'll hit her with the big one: "What's most important in life?" She smiled, "Loving everybody." Nice, but a tough pill for a cynic like me. So, a question to which only someone her age could provide an informed answer, "Do you recommend longevity?" She gave me a knowing look, "Yes, indeed. I'm looking forward to

100." My money's on her. Any final words of wisdom? "Everything will work out for the best if you just leave it alone." I said good-bye, and left her alone.

> *There may be little or much beyond the grave,*
> *But the strong are saying nothing until they see.*

> —ROBERT FROST (1874-1963)

## A LETTER NEVER SENT

*Dear James:*

*As you know I have been doing a lot of research on this book, delving back to earliest recorded thoughts and communications of mankind, and I have been struck with the similarity of ideas and ruminations throughout our history to present. While technology and physical exploration have advanced greatly over the years, philosophy and the musings of minds great and small as to the meaning of it all have remained stationary. Similar thoughts about life and death have been repeated throughout time, expressed differently in many languages, examined from many angles, presented with many clever spins and phraseologies, but with no more insight, depth of vision or wisdom than before. Dot's funeral is a case in point. Because she had been a teacher for so many years, there was an unusual age spread among the many people in atten-*

dance. There were the old hands who had already been to too many funerals and the youngsters who were experiencing their first. There was concern and sympathy for you (her husband of fifty-five years) and for other family members. There were all the close friends who wanted to (and in many cases did) help and the preacher who wanted to assure everybody that Dot had led a good life and had ascended to heaven and was now in a better place. And everyone agreed that it was good her long illness had finally come to its peaceful conclusion. But there was also the undeniable undercurrent, especially among those over sixty, of who's next? and when me? Is there really that peaceful place to go to and will I be able to go there too? The preacher reached deep to find the best that the Bible has to offer on the subject. Words like "faith, love, peace, eternal, believe, Holy Spirit, perpetual light and heaven" were used to smooth the occasion and prevent words like "doubt, gone, termination and black void" from surfacing. What was going on in the minds of all those people? Where was the wisdom for such a special moment? Everyone was aware that time wasn't going to stop with that ceremony. Everyone there, from the youngest to the eldest, would move on toward their own intimate rendezvous with eternity. Knowing that may not be wisdom, but it is what we humans are left with.

*Your brother-in-law and friend*

❧

# SUICIDE

*Humpty Dumpty sat on a wall,*
*Humpty Dumpty had a great fall.*
*All the king's horses*
*And all the king's men,*
*Couldn't put Humpty together again.*

(Though there are no records that prove conclusively that Mr. Dumpty took his own life, there is certainly plenty of room for speculation. Either way, he is fondly remembered by his many friends and associates as being a good egg. )

Almost everyone over sixty has a suicide plan, though few of us actually carry it out. It can be comforting to have such a plan all arranged there in the back of your head so that you know if things get tough, beyond bearing, there's always a way out. The catch-22 is that by the time things get beyond bearing, we are usually no longer physically able to execute ourselves. We must rely on others to understand our plight and come to our aid. This is why everyone needs a living will so that family, friends, doctors, hospitals and lawyers (all should have copies) will see to it that our desire to be rescued from a prolonged, painful, expensive death—without-dignity—is carried out.

> *To be, or not to be—that is the question.*
>
> —WILLIAM SHAKESPEARE, *Hamlet* (1603)

Suicide would not seem to be for the young, the well adjusted, the moneyed, the healthy or the happy. But this is often not the case. In fact according to statistics from the U. S. Department of Health and Human Services, the largest number of suicides takes place among 25 to 44 year olds. There are far more suicides among 15 to 24 year olds than 55 to 74 year olds! These figures are based on 1995 numbers and could change as the senior population continues to grow at a faster rate than other age groups. Another factor could be that those with the strongest suicidal tendencies have already done away with themselves well before the onset of old age.

> *Some made the long drop from the apartment or the office window; some took it quietly in two-car garages with the motor running; some used the native tradition of*

*the Colt or Smith and Wesson; those well-constructed*
*implements that end insomnia, terminate remorse, cure*
*cancer, avoid bankruptcy and blast an exit from*
*intolerable positions by the pressure of a finger . . .*

—ERNEST HEMINGWAY, *To Have and Have Not* (1934)

I bought a book once that dealt with how best to do away with yourself. Not that I was planning anything that drastic. I suppose it was just morbid curiosity that made me want to read it. At any rate, it was a great disappointment. It described only very complex ways of ending it all when, to me at least, and certainly to Mr. Hemingway, it's simply not all that complicated. Hemingway did it nineteen days before what would have been his 62nd birthday "by the pressure of a finger," but not with a Smith and Wesson or a Colt. He selected a doubled-barreled Boss shotgun with a full choke. According to his biographer Carlos Baker in *Ernest Hemingway A Life Story,* in the dawn hours of a lovely early July morning in 1961 he loaded both barrels, placed the butt of the gun solidly on the floor and positioned his forehead against both barrel openings. Then he activated the triggers. Messy method, but the outcome is never in doubt.

*It is not worth the bother of killing yourself,*
*since you always kill yourself too late.*

—E. M. CIORANH, *The Trouble with Being Born* (1973)

One birth; one death; no exceptions. It is the fact that we know that there is no escape from death that makes suicide so popular. Got to die anyway, why not do it now, get it out of the way, skip all the pain and tribulation in between? Toward the end of life this decision becomes easier, the reasons for an immediate death more compelling. With one determined action you can save yourself pain and suffering, save your heirs money, possibly a great deal of it. Who has the time to care for the terminally ill? Who has the money? Trouble is your children and grandchildren still love you and want you to hang on and don't want the guilt that would be associated with anything less than a total effort to save you for as long as possible. But the time comes . . . the time comes. At some point it is clear that you have no viable future. But, if you are on life support and it's time to pull the plug, you are in no position to pull it yourself. All this has to have been discussed and determined (in writing) much earlier with your children or whoever are the responsible persons. With death so close, the legal and moral boundaries between natural death, suicide and even murder become intermingled and blurred. Someone who loves you has to have the guts to step up, do the right thing and end it.

> *If through practice of insight you develop a sense of ease,*
> *then time has no relevance. If you're miserable,*
> *time does matter. It's so unbearable, so enormous*
> *you want to get out of it as soon as possible.*
>
> —THE DALAI LAMA,
> quoted in *The Washington Post* (1998)

Suicide is not for sissies. But you do need a better reason than just general unhappiness or having a bad day. Unhappiness can be turned around by a chance event or meeting. Bad days can become good days. The excuse for suicide needs to be an unalterable condition that promises unbearable pain and misery. When all roads lead in unacceptable directions, then you may have to consider self-destruction. When suicide is the best option you have, then you may have to face that reality and follow where it leads.

> *Razors pain you;*
> *Rivers are damp;*
> *Acids stain you;*
> *And drugs cause cramp.*

*Guns aren't lawful;*
*Nooses give;*
*Gas smells awful;*
*You might as well live.*

—DOROTHY PARKER, "Résumé" (1926)

---

## A LETTER NEVER SENT

*Dear Tom:*
*To answer your question, yes, I have a plan. When the going*
*gets tough, the tough get going—right out of town; right out of*
*this world! Because sometimes the going can get tougher than*
*any human soul can take no matter how tough. So, I have a*
*plan, though I doubt it can ever be carried out because by the*
*time the pain is that overwhelming, it is usually already too*
*late. But my plan is a nice, simple one. I saw a movie once*
*where the action took place in the future and there were*
*these rooms you could go to when you got ready. You would*
*walk in and lie down on a comfortable platform and watch*
*beautiful nature scenes on a large screen and the profession-*
*als there would see to it that you would die quietly and in*
*peace. My plan incorporates only some of this. I get in my old*
*1969 Bronco and drive down to the end of the lake where I*

can look back and see my house on the hill, a pretty view full of pleasant memories and good times past. Then I run the hose from the tail pipe through the window and seal up all the cracks with duct tape. I take my seat behind the wheel, pour myself a lovely cold martini from the pitcher and pour one for Anne if she is joining me. We pop some tranquilizers along with the booze and then I crank up the engine. We hold hands as we slip into eternity. What's your plan?

Your Friend

# FOOD

*Jack Sprat could eat no fat,*
*His wife could eat no lean,*
*And so between them both, you see,*
*They licked the platter clean.*

(Though illustrations invariably show Jack as skinny and Mrs. Sprat as portly, the more modern theory is that Jack was actually too heavy and had cholesterol and blood pressure problems so he could "eat no fat." Mrs. S. was too thin and anemic and under Doctor's orders to "lick the platter clean.")

After sixty, many of us are urged to watch what we eat. We are either advised to eat more, or to eat less. We are told, if not by our doctors then by our local TV "news" stations, not to eat foods with saturated fat, or those high in cholesterol and *to* eat foods high in fiber, rich in vitamins and minerals. On other TV shows, or on alternating days on the same channels, we are instructed that a certain amount of saturated fat is necessary, that some cholesterol is good, that too much fiber can cause stomach discomfort, and that certain people must beware of certain vitamins and minerals. Fortunately, while we watch and listen to all this, most of us have the good sense to go on eating pretty much as we always have. Because the TV information is based on statistics which are based on surveys which are based on "controlled" observations of groups of people over time, such statistic have the nasty habit of contradicting themselves. It is a fact that more two legged men have heart attacks than men with but a single limb. But, having a leg amputated is not recommended to preserve a sound heart. At least not yet.

*Eat to live, and not live to eat.*
—BENJAMIN FRANKLIN, *Poor Richard's Almanac* (1733)
(perhaps first stated by Socrates —469-399 B.C.)

As we get older meals take on more importance, possibly because other things grow less important. We think too much and talk too much about food. We study restaurant menus as if they were international treaties, and we discuss and examine each entry as if our selection were going to impact world peace. The most important thing on the menu is usually the price.

*Do I dare eat a peach?*

—T. S. ELLIOT, *The Love Song of J. Alfred Prufrock* (1917)

Doctor's orders prevent too many of us from eating the things we enjoy most. Sooner or later this happens to almost everybody. So if you have not yet had your diet restricted, hurry up and eat plenty of the good stuff. Shake on the salt. Eat a warm doughnut with your strong black coffee. Dredge your crab meat in real melted butter. Have your steaks thick and rare with deep fried onion rings on the side. Eat ice cream snuggled up close to your peach pie. Don't even think about tomorrow. Tomorrow may be a gastronomic Sahara.

*God sends meat and the Devil sends cooks.*

—ENGLISH PROVERB

Think about this: when you boil vegetables much of what is good ends up in the water; when you boil meat, much of what is bad ends up in the water. Hmm. Maybe that's why most of us don't eat that much boiled food, and why vegetables are probably better for you than meat no matter how you cook them.

*To a man with an empty stomach, food is god.*

—MOHANDAS (MAHATMA) GANDHI (1869-1948)

Like a number of other human functions, eating is necessary to life. Unlike breathing, excreting, and a survivable environment, eating has become an art form for many. So much so, in fact, that some of us quite forget that we are eating because we must, not just because we enjoy it. But the poor know, and the aged know. The truly poor will eat anything that will help them live another day. Many elderly eat because they are forced to; some literally forced to through a feeding tube inserted directly into their stomachs. Under these circumstances words such as "cuisine" and "gourmet" seem trivial.

*What is food to one, is to others bitter poison.*

—TITUS LUCRETIUS CARUS,
*De Rerum Natura* (99-55 BC)

Some of the foods we bite can bite back. Allergic reactions to such foods as strawberries, shrimp, peanuts and dairy products, are only a part of an amazing list that grows and grows as we age and age. The list of the good things we can eat, only dwindles.

*Some hae meat and canna eat,*
*And some wad eat that want it;*
*But we hae meat, and we can eat,*
*And sae the Lord be thankit.*

—ROBERT BURNS (1759-96)

---

## A LETTER NEVER SENT

*Dear Bo:*
*Remember the time in Greenport when that lobster you were*
*working on went flying out of your buttery grasp, landing on*
*the table next to us? Or that time in Paris when you made*
*the reservation under the name "Monet" and the maitre d'*
*practically swooned when we arrived, chanting "Ah, Monsieur*
*Monet! Monsieur Monet!" as he swept us to our table? Yes*
*indeed eating good food in good places has always been big*
*with us. Not fancy food in fancy places, mind you, or nouveau*
*food in some suave joint with three seatings, but stuff that*
*really tastes good in a comfortable setting. There are plenty of*
*such places on the side streets of Paris and New Orleans and*
*New York and so many other cities. Trouble is, who wants to go*
*to a city at this stage of the game. Jackets and ties? Forget it.*
*But, thinking back to those expense-account days, I can still*
*recall a lot of specific dishes and settings and tastes. Maybe*

*we should try to swing a major loan and go back to Venice and eat until the money runs out. Everything might not taste quite as good as the first time around, but it would surely taste better than what we had for dinner last night. And those views would be as great as ever.*

*Your Friend*

# RELIGION

*There I met an old man,*
*Who wouldn't say his prayers.*
*I took him by the left leg*
*And threw him down the stairs.*

(It is actions such as this that tend to give religion a bad name.)

In the latter part of our lives almost all of us give some thought to the possibilities of after life and this leads us to consider religion. For those fortunate enough to have been deeply religious for most of their lives, no change is necessary. Keep the faith and you will find comfort in your belief that you will sooner or later go to your reward. For the unlucky ones who have too many questions to be blindly faithful, eternity stretches out vastly before us without including us. Some seek a quick fix and "find the one and only true God." The rest of us, I fear, will drop into the abyss when our time comes.

*"Sensible men are all of the same religion.' 'And pray, what is
that?' inquired the prince. 'Sensible men never tell.'*

—BENJAMIN DISRAELI, *Endymion* (1880)

The world and its environs are a puzzle that man has been
attempting to solve with only limited success for approxi-
mately two million years. Since (at the moment) humans
seem to be the overwhelmingly most important thing on the
face of the Earth, we tend to see and interpret everything in
terms of ourselves. Still there is a great deal that we can neither interpret nor understand so we explain much of this
phenomena with our various world religions that feature an
almighty icon, sometimes called God. God is most often a
super-human who resides in a mystical place and who created the world and the humans who dwell therein. The subjects of these various "gods" are required to believe in them
(almost always a "him") through blind faith. Each "god" also
comes complete with certain rules of human behavior which
vary somewhat from religion to religion. This divergence can
cause conflict among believers of the various sects. So much
so that they frequently get in a frenzy and kill one another
all knowing with certainty that the one and only true "god"
was on their side, and after their death they will be rewarded
with some form of eternal prize.

*Religion . . . is the opium of the people.*

—KARL MARX (1844)

After sixty we all tend to take a very hard look at what religions have to offer, and if we are convinced that one promises everlasting life, we become happy converts. But if we are not convinced, we must grit our teeth and face oblivion. All other choices seem hypocritical.

*All the great things we know have come to us from neurotics. It is they and only they who have founded religions and created great works of art.*

—MARCEL PROUST (1871-1922)

What each individual is required to determine for himself (no help, please) is only which "god" is the real God. The rewards and penalties are simple: choose right and you get life everlasting, choose wrong and you face eternal damnation, or at the very least, oblivion. All human beings are aware of these choices. You look at God; I look at God; she looks at God. Trouble is we do not necessarily see the same thing. Individual choice, interpretation and tradition color our perception. While we all may actually be looking at the same God, most of us cannot agree that this could possibly be so.

*I don't adhere to rabbis, preachers, evangelists, all of that. I've learned more from the songs than I've learned from any of this kind of entity. The songs are my lexicon. I believe the songs.*

—BOB DYLAN, in an interview by David Gates,
*Newsweek* (1997)

If you know that at one point in time something began, then you can reasonably expect that at later a point it will end. It then follows that the only thing that will last forever, must have existed forever. If such an eternal thing exists— and it is as hard to imagine that it could, as to imagine that it couldn't—then that thing can be called God. He is the answer to all those questions that seem to have no answers. As long as the questions exist, then God exists. The problems develop when various religions want to claim Him for their very own. It seems to me that God exists with or without religions. In other words, God can probably do just fine on His own with or without all the hocus-pocus beamed up at him from Earth. God does not need us; we need Him. That is why we cry out to him in times of desperation. Whether or not he ever answers is open to Earthly debate.

*I shall never believe that God plays dice with the world.*

—ALBERT EINSTEIN (1879-1955)
*Einstein, His Life and Times* by Phillip Frank

## A LETTER NEVER SENT

*Dear Lorraine:*

*You attend church more than any atheist I know. I guess like the rest of us you are seeking but probably not finding. If you do find, please call ... collect. I guess it's just hard to imagine not existing anymore. I'm not at all sure there's not a god, it's just that religions have so confused the issue that it is just about impossible to cut through all the crap to get a clean look. All the religions are more concerned with making up the rules than with what God might be and what He might be up to. Anyway, it's hard for me to understand that someone can be as blindly faithful in the rightness of the Democratic party as you are, and can't find some religion to fall for. I mean, an independent like myself has some excuse.*

*Your Friend*

# Now

*Rain, rain, go away,*
*Come again another day*

(We know we need rain, but we never want it to rain now.)

It takes a strong insightful person to choose future results over present satisfaction. There is a test they give to young children. They seat a child at a table and place a single marshmallow in front of him or her. The child is then told that he or she can eat the marshmallow now or wait a few minutes; the child receives a second marshmallow as a reward for waiting. Some children can't wait, others can. Research reportedly reveals that those children who wait make the more successful adults. Children, of course, have a much longer span of now (or time) to work with than those of us over sixty. We would probably be best advised to devour the marshmallow immediately.

*Ah, take the cash and let the credit go,*

*Nor heed the rumble of a distant Drum.*

—OMAR KHAYYAM, *Rubaiyat* (11-12th c.)

Trans. Edward FitzGerald (1859)

Now is where we constantly are, and so it takes precedence over the past and even the future. When we itch, there are times when we absolutely have to scratch. Now is the present which is the result of past actions and the cause of future actions (which quickly become more results). But for such an all-important aspect of our lives, the present is forever elusive and can only be captured on film or tape or in often inadequate words that struggle to represent it. These images exist to remind us that the past was at one time the present, and it was, as far as anyone can tell, real.

*Tomorrow do thy worst, for I have lived today.*

—JOHN DRYDEN, *Imitation of Horace* (1697)

A marble Abraham Lincoln sits in Washington D.C. to be seen and remembered and revered. But, he signs no new legislation. His council can only be sought in books. His eyes do not see, his hands are cold. Lincoln long ago ran out of earthly nows, as we all will . . . or already have. Only death can turn now into forever.

*All our yesterdays are summarized in our now,*
*and all the tomorrows are ours to shape.*

—Hal Borland, *The Tomorrows—December 30* (1964)

There are two ways to regard now. One, as that less-than-a-millisecond flash that comes and goes in the same moment —like a single note in a symphony. It is revealed in the re-run highlights of Sunday's big games. No matter how painful it is for some to watch, the ball is always fumbled in exactly the same way. Even such recent errors (or triumphs) are firmly glued in the past.

*Nothing is there to come, and nothing past,*
*But an eternal now does always last.*

—Abraham Crowley, *Davideis* (1656)

The other way to consider now is as a permanent point that never moves, like the rock in a stream that the water flows over and around. Now never stops being now, so it exists forever as the dividing point where the future becomes the past. So, when we want to "make our mark," or "be remembered," or "make this moment last," what we really want is to own a chunk of now for as long as humanly possible.

*. . . nothing startles me beyond the moment.*

—JOHN KEATS (letter-1817)

Sometimes one now may seem to last longer than another. When we're sick or in pain time stretches endlessly. Sex and ice cream moments may be gone in a lick. Fear, always lurking in the background of our minds, comes leaping to the forefront when imminent danger presents itself and that particular now threatens to be our last.

*The present contains nothing more than the past, and what is found in the effect was already in the cause.*

—HENRI BERGSON, *Creative Evolution* (1907)

Do we really exist? The answer would seem to be, "Well, of course we do." But if we do exist, then we must exist in the present, or now. The future is whatever lies ahead, a place we can never actually reach because the moment we arrive, the future has become the present. The future is unattainable, always tantalizingly beyond our grasp. The future can only exist conceptually in our minds. The past, on the other hand, lies behind us. We have been there, but when we were there it was not the past at all, it was the present. So while evidence of the past is all around us, to actually exist in the past would require some sort of time travel and that is one machine that has not yet been invented. All of which leaves us with the present, or now. But, every time we attempt to hold on to the present it becomes something else. In actuality it is as elusive as the future and the past. By the time you say "now," now has already become then. So, if the present, or now, doesn't actually exist, we are compelled to wonder again, do we really exist?

*The future is a deceitful time that always says to us, 'Not Yet,' and thus denies us. The future is not the time of love: what man truly wants he wants now.*

—OCTAVIO PAZ , *Postscript* (1970)

## A LETTER NEVER SENT

*Dear Ted:*

*That job interview you gave me back in 1956 still sticks in my mind. How much that one meeting directed the course of my life. It was what they call a defining moment. Every life has such moments that, however brief, have a major impact. We call them "forks in the road" or "being in the right place at the right time." Then years passed and you retired and I retired and yet we are friends still. Our friendship has given us the illusion of an extended moment in the present. We are friends today, were friends yesterday, will be friends tomorrow. We have stretched time out over the years and hope to stretch it some more. And all the stuff we did together lives again when we talk about it, laugh about it, cry about it. As long as we can keep it going, it all appears to be just one great big extended now that we will enjoy for a while longer. So let's tip our caps to the moment back in '56 when you loomed so large behind that desk.*

*Your Friend*

# LONGEVITY

*There was an old woman*
*Lived under a hill;*
*And if she's not gone,*
*She lives there still.*

(And if she is gone it's probably because the kids sent her off to the  local rest home and moved in under the hill themselves.)

The aging process, getting older one day at a time, is so gradual that most of us don't really think much about it until we reach certain milestones, such as thirty, forty or fifty. Then at some point, as we see seventy looming, we perceive what so many millions before us have come to know, that instead of "they" being old, it is "us" who are now the ancient ones.

*Grow old along with me!*
*The best is yet to be,*
*The last of life, for which the first was made.*

—ROBERT BROWNING, *Babbi Ben Ezra* (1812-89)

Many believe that if life could be lived backwards, it would be an improvement. At first glance the vision of growing younger day by day, rather than older, has great appeal. The talk would be all about "saving up for our youth," and "trying to grow young gracefully." Our spouses would look better year by year. Our appetites would improve. New strength would flow into our limbs and our libidos. Our golf scores would actually improve as time went on. People in the hair transplant business would want for customers. Cosmetic surgeons would be on the bread line. Many of us would want to look "old and respectable" for as long as possible. We would certainly not want to look "young beneath our years."

*Every man desires to live long, but no man would be old.*
—JONATHAN SWIFT, *Thoughts on Various Subjects* (1711)

On the other hand, if we were to live life backwards, we would in no way escape oblivion. It would just lurk at the opposite end of the scale. Instead of dying, we would simply become unborn. We would select our spouses when we were both old, trying to choose one that would "improve with youth." Then, with great pride, we would watch our companion grow more and more physically attractive until at last we would be children again and could no longer comprehend what all the fuss was about. June-December romances could become living nightmares as child molestation could cause the necessary legal separation of long-married couples. The possibilities are too confusing to envision. Let's just forget this whole reverse concept and go back to dealing with forward motion again. Make that s-l-o-w motion, if you please.

> . . . *many experts believe . . . that healthy babies born today*
> *will likely live a full century, and their children*
> *may live to see 120 or beyond.*
>
> —JOHN BARRY, *The Miami Herald* (1998)

With the birthrate increasing as well as longevity increasing, the old seem no longer willing to make room for the young and the Earth is getting over crowded. It's like a theater where the matinee viewers won't leave their seats for the evening ticket holders. Pretty soon, someone is going to have to shout "Fire!" The population of the world is expected to double in the next fifty years! According to "The World Almanac" (1998) about 59,000 Americans currently fall into the formerly exclusive centenarian group, people one hundred years old or more. This number is expected to soar astronomically in the coming years. Experts predict that by the year 2050 our health system will be dealing with two million baby boomers turning one hundred. What's it going to take for our leaders to face up to the exploding population problem and consider ways to deal with it?

*I think you are going to live to be an old, old woman—with me. And die on the same day and be buried in the same grave. That would be lovely.*

—DAME AGATHA CHRISTIE,
*A Murder Is Announced* (1890-1976)

A 79-year-old woman told me the other day that she would never die. Of course, she was a healthy specimen, active physically and mentally and had trouble comprehending anyone who was not. Why not live forever as long as the food remains delicious, the body functional, the brain sharp, and all the senses acute. The well and well adjusted have no need to die, but die they will. If their luck holds, the end will come unrecognized in a dream. If luck and good health abandon them, there will be a dramatic change in attitude. Death, not longevity, is the friend of the old and infirm.

*I don't have a warm personal enemy left. They've all died off. I miss them terribly because they helped define me.*

—CLAIR BOOTH LUCE (1903-1989)

Humans, especially Americans, are no longer willing to leave their longevity to the whim of the gods. Everyday on our TV sets, magazines, newspapers, best selling books and the internet, we are bombarded with advice on what to eat, how to exercise, best ways to handle stress. In short, advice on how to live longer and longer lives. All we need to do is follow the often conflicting advice of Oprah or some other small screen oracle, and we will stay alive practically forever and look better doing it. Not that there might not be something to all these tips. We actually are living longer. But I don't think even the *New England Journal of Medicine* wants to venture how many of us are enjoying the ride all the way to the last stop.

> *Like anybody, I would like to live a long life.*
> *Longevity has its place.*
>
> —MARTIN LUTHER KING, JR. (1968)

No matter what, the death rate always remains constant; one per customer.

> *'Tis very certain the desire of life*
> *Prolongs it.*
>
> —LORD BYRON, "Don Juan" (1819-24)

## A LETTER NEVER SENT

*Dear George:*

*Another birthday—another year farther away from something
and closer to something. We remember past birthday celebra-
tions especially when we were in Africa (at Samburu that year,
right?) and you were but fifty (hamsini in Swahili) and Anne
and I gave you that silver half dollar from the year of your
birth (hamsini years, hamsini cents, how clever). We were all
on an African high, so elevated, in fact, I can still feel it these
dozen years later. When something is as good as those trips
were, they at first lift you and then when you think you will
never get back, they lean on you, especially when the theme
from "Out Of Africa" plays. Sentimental, of course. (Why does
sentimental have such a bad name? Because we all feel it
and are ashamed to admit our weakness?) We need fresh
plans. We will return and in so saying we can focus our attention on the future. No more maudlin tears, only smiles of
anticipation. The rule of climbing is, "Don't look down." The rule
of aging is, "Don't look back," and . . . keep on climbing.*

*Your Friend*

༺❀༻

# Strong Drink

*This little piggy went to market,*
*This little piggy stayed home,*
*This little piggy had roast beef,*
*This little piggy had none.*
*And this little piggy cried,*
*'Wee, wee, wee,' all the way home!*

(It's pretty clear which little piggy had stopped
off at "Joe's" on the way home.)

At no matter what age, there are only two kinds of drinking: responsible and irresponsible—fun and no fun. Amazingly, some people can live very long lives abusing alcohol all the way. But more often they die before their time of cardiovascular, cancer, liver or pancreas diseases. Excessive alcohol intake may also result in harmful effects on the brain and nervous system. The list of the different kinds of possible, if not probable, damage to your innards goes on and on. And, of course, drunk driving can result in tragedy for the innocent as well as the perpetrator. On the other hand, responsible drinking can lift the spirits, increase social activities and inject a pleasant interlude into a busy or drab day.

*I always keep a supply of stimulant handy in case I*
*see a snake—which I also keep handy.*

—W. C. Fields (1880-1946)

As we can see from the above, W. C. Fields (W. C. for William Claude) made it to sixty-six, not bad for a man with a nose like that. There are many celebrity drinkers who lived well into their sixties and beyond. For example, John Barrymore very much liked his booze and still he managed to (just) qualify for inclusion here by making it to sixty. He is quoted as saying about a late acquaintance, "He neither drank, smoked nor rode a bicycle. Living frugally, saving his money, he died early, surrounded by greedy relatives. It was a great lesson for me." A more recent example, Dean Martin, whose reportedly heavy drinking may have been exaggerated, lived into his late seventies. He once said, "You are not drunk if you can lie on the floor without holding on."

*Oh, Georgia booze is mighty fine booze,*
*The best yuh ever poured yuh,*

*But it eats the soles right offen your shoes,*
*For Hell's broke loose in Georgia*

—STEVEN VINCENT BENÉT,
*The Mountain Whippoorwill* (1923)

The strength of the booze we drink should lessen over time. This is because of lessons learned through the school of hard knocks or chugs ("I drank the whole bottle last time and fell over, so this time I'll only drink half the bottle.") and because of the diminished capacity of our aging bodies to handle the side effects of strong drink. Martini's, Manhattans, stingers and their ilk are seldom offered or accepted by the over sixty clan. Same with cordials. Nowadays I'd as soon swallow battery acid as Drambuie. Whiskey and water is the order of the day with emphasis on the water. The after-sixty version of a martini is gin with water and ice and four or five olives. Sip slowly. Wine is fine; beer, (one or two a day) never fear. The latest research on how much alcohol can actually be good for you indicates that one drink will provide maximum benefits. More booze does not produce more benefits (damn!). What to drink? The belief that red wine will provide more benefits than whiskey is pooh-poohed. But like all medical advice dispensed by the media, this could change. My advice is, limit yourself to one or two cocktails (1½ ounces of 80-proof whiskey per drink) and you can enjoy a relaxed cocktail hour without doing yourself any harm. A third light drink (which I call "a rare") may be sipped on special occasions such as your 70th birthday. Cheers!

> *Show me the way to go home.*
> *I'm tired and I want to go to bed.*
> *I had a little drink about an hour ago,*
> *And it went right to my head.*
>
> —OLD COLLEGE DRINKING SONG

> *Indicate the way to my abode.*
> *I'm fatigued and I wish to retire.*
> *I had a little beverage 60 minutes ago,*
> *And it went right to my cerebellum.*
>
> —GENTLEMAN'S VERSION

A drinking friend, now diseased, beseeched me one evening after much imbibing at several New York City watering spots, "Take me to my beddie." Drinking at our age is preferably done close to home, if not at home. As time slides by on the one-to-ten scale, drinking moves from five to four to three and bed time from seven to eight to nine.

Drinking becomes a before dinner thing and perhaps a glass of wine with. But, after the meal, the mattress looms large. A soft pillow or two, a good mystery, a bedside table with a bright reading light—these are the comforts that cap the bottle with the glorious prospect of a no-hangover tomorrow.

> . . . *my medical advisors have warned me it may well*
> *be unwise to give up alcohol at my age.*
> —CHIEF INSPECTOR MORSE, "Death Is Now My Neighbor"
> by Colin Dexter (1996)

You, too, may recall this wonderful story about Sir Winston Churchill, a serious statesman and drinker, who lived to the extended age of ninety-one. One night upon leaving a restaurant in London he encountered an unattractive woman just entering. "You, Madam," he is reported to have said, "Are exceedingly ugly." "Sir," she gasped, "You are exceedingly drunk." To which Churchill replied, his wit undulled by imbibing, "True, Madam, but in the morning I shall be sober."

> *The worst thing about some men is that*
> *when they are not drunk they are sober.*
> —WILLIAM BUTLER YEATS( 1865-1939)

While it is unarguably true that overly imbibing is bad, it is equally true that not imbibing at all is not good. There are those who don't drink or no longer drink because of doctor's orders or because they are recovering alcoholics. This is good and proper. But generally speaking we must consider the voluntary teetotaler in the same light as the vegetarian and born-again evangelist. These people are extremists and extremists are trouble and usually no fun at all. Now I do know a few (very few) people over sixty who abstain and also have a sense of humor. All rules have exceptions. But one thing life-long teetotalers don't have is a bag full of hilarious old drinking stories to swap during the cocktail hour.

*Here's looking at you, kid.*
—JULIUS J. EPSTEIN, screenwriter, *Casablanca* (1942)

## A LETTER NEVER SENT

*Dear Bobby:*
*Long, long time no see. You were one of my earliest friends and when we got to be about sixteen, one of my first drinking buddies. So was Frankie. (Is Frankie somewhere in that great*

big saloon-in-the-sky with you?) I fondly remember you as a tall, blond, strapping guy, always a smile, very bright. Tough competition between the two of us for certain girls, especially Bar Nash. Neither of us won that race. Didn't see as much of you since we went to different universities and then the service. You asked me to be an usher in your wedding party, but my C. O. wouldn't let me off. And then later, when I was working in New York and you had your law degree, you showed up at my office looking and smelling real bad with a check you couldn't get cashed so I helped you out. Then one other time I saw you, and then never more. The booze got you just as it got Frank and a lot of other people I used to know. The rest of us tapered off and we made it to sixty and many of us are still counting and still sipping. One beer at noon, two light highballs in the evening. Very pleasant. Seemingly very benign, except for those legions who didn't know how to stop counting at two.

*Still Your Friend*

# WHAT'S NEW

*Lavender's blue, dilly dilly, lavender's green;*
*When I am king, dilly dilly, you shall be queen.*

(What's new about this nursery rhyme is really very silly.
It's just that "remarkable" is what is meant by "dilly." I
looked it up in Webster's, so I would not abuse it, But now
that I'm enlightened, I'll probably never use it.)

New is a word that recedes as a life goes on. New is
also a word with the power to rejuvenate as in:
"How's that new grand baby of yours?" New is a
word with a future, and for those of us concerned with
diminishing futures, new belongs in there with hope and
life and love. For those with a philosophical turn of mind, it
sometimes seems as if nothing is new. The big eternal questions have always been there. And, new can be disagree-
able, such as new wrinkles, glasses, pains, illnesses We all
change every day and every day itself is new and brings
with it fresh experiences even though they may seem to be

repetitious. Repetition can only continue so long. If you do twenty pushups each morning (no, I don't) then each pushup has a number, an intensity and an individuality (you never know which one will bring on the heart attack, for example). It's like shooting baskets from the foul line. Each one seems to be exactly the same, but the fact is that even when done by a pro, some go in and some do not. Each shot is a new opportunity with an uncertain result. Each moment in time, each day we live, is one we have never lived before and is, therefore, new.

*Neither do men put new wine into old bottles.*

—Matthew 9:17

An individual human being is a perishable product. Our vast medical research institutes and drug companies are cranking day and night to discover new ways to extend our life spans and improve the quality of our lives, and they are being successful. We now live longer than ever before. Don't be misguided and think that this is some huge altruistic, humanitarian project. Not so. It's about selling new, more expensive pills and other types of treatments. It's about the bottom line. But, hey, don't get angry, get even. Invest in the common stocks of Merck, Pfizer and Abbott Labs. Get sick; get well; make money.

*To mourne a mischief that is past and gone*
*Is the next way to draw new mischief on.*

—WILLIAM SHAKESPEARE, *Othello* (1604-05)

The newest of the new is Technology. Over sixty or not, there is no escaping its impact, both the plus and the minus. We all must deal with it because it confronts us in our homes, on the phone, on the TV, in our automobiles and even on (or in) our persons in the form of wrist watches, pagers and pacemakers. Everything comes up computers and chips. They are pervasive. Perhaps all these rapid changes during our lifetimes have conditioned us older Americans to treat new and different as commonplace, and have emboldened us to try new and different in other areas of our living. All of us may be old dogs, but nowadays, as we check our e-mail each morning for messages from our grandchildren, we are learning whole bagfuls of new tricks.

*Forever piping songs forever new.*

—JOHN KEATS, *Ode on a Grecian Ern* (1820)

Everything was new at one time. While something can only prove its value over time, that does not mean we should consider it valueless just because it is new. But a lot of supposedly "new" stuff is not really new. The importance of popular music, for example, is its impact on a generation or two, not its newness. Given the long view, swing is no newer than jazz; hard rock is no newer than the waltz. All generational music is doomed to essentially die out with its generation. Think of the cutting edge as the slicing of a bottomless cake. The slicing knife having cut moves on to continue cutting endlessly. In the long view, new is merely the constant prelude to old.

*What is valuable is not new, and what is new is not valuable.*

—HENRY PETER BROUGHAM (1778-1868)

Time, distance, death, take from us old friends. We can remember them and the good times past, but that is of little help when it comes to our enjoyment of the present. We have a need for newness in our lives. We go to the movies, watch the tube, read the latest novels, magazines and newspapers, all in an effort to stay current. There is that feeling that to lose touch with contemporary happenings would be to lose our place in the present and to slide slowly away with the rest of the past. It is symbolic that time turns us gray and we all begin to resemble faded photographs. The old sport buys himself a new red convertible and feels young again, never mind the neighbors who mumble, "The old fool." The old fool is merely trying his damnedest to stay alive. Pinch him; he's still for real.

> *The world would be a safer place,*
> *If someone had a plan,*
> *Before exploring Outer Space,*
> *To find the inner man.*
>
> —EDGAR Y. HARBURG (1898-1981)

## A LETTER NEVER SENT

*Dear Jennifer:*

*I can remember driving you and Joyce around many years ago and both of you complaining that I was playing "old people's music" on the car radio. Now with your kids apt to request rap instead of rock, it's about to happen to you, which is of course to me sweet poetic justice. (I never had the chance to complain to my father even though I liked Sinatra and he liked Strauss because in those days few people had car radios.) Kids embrace the newness of everything. From haircuts to clothes to music, they alter it from the previous generation and then claim it as their own. It's a sort of club membership thing. New is in, old is out, which for those of us who are actually old, is a bit of a kick in the teeth. Words like unwanted and discarded come readily to mind. One thing I enjoyed about my job was that it brought me constantly in contact with the young people in the office making me feel "up to date" and "with it." From my daily association with them I could talk the talk. Of course television also enables us to keep up with the latest jargon; that is if we can bear to watch the daily vomiting of so many mediocre-to-awful sit-coms. (I can't.) So, what may appear to be new is really nothing more than soon-to-be-old in disguise. It strikes me that what is really new, and has been over the centuries, is exploration. Man's insatiable curiosity and quest for new frontiers has now led us into space. The planets and stars, it seems to me, are our real destiny and my own curiosity makes me want to stick around to find out just how far we will go. Presumably you'll be able to learn a lot more of that great endeavor than I will, and Allison will see beyond that. Her children, who knows? We individual human beings are just steps in a stair-way leading upward to the unknown. I'm glad that you and I were able to spend so many years climbing together.*

*Your Loving Father*

# CONTEMPORARIES

*London Bridge is falling down,*
*Falling down, falling down,*
*London Bridge is falling down,*
*My fair lady.*

(We're all falling, falling, falling down together, my fair lady,
but some of us ain't quite all the way down yet!)

People are living longer, and getting older, which means, to those of us over sixty, while we are indeed older than we ever were before, we are not as much older as we would have been fifty years ago. Science has tacked a few more years on to our lives. The median age in this country (half over, half under) is the oldest it has ever been —34.9 years old in 1997 according to U.S. Dept. of Commerce figures, and that number seems destined to continue to grow. In 1920 the median age was only 25.3. Today more of us are living more years. Senior power has become a reality which will bring more clout to the "cane mutiny."

*A man lives not only his personal life, as an individual,*
*but also, consciously or unconsciously, the life of his*
*epoch and his contemporaries.*

—THOMAS MANN, *The Magic Mountain* (1924)

There's a wonderful old restaurant/bar in South Miami called "Fox's." You can sit there in the semi-darkness, listening to Sinatra or Jo Stafford, sipping a drink, eating a steak, knowing that this is one place that hasn't changed much in over forty or fifty years. A lot of white-headed people eat there or imbibe at the rail and it's easy to understand their conversations because we are mostly all contemporaries. We know about The Mills Brothers and The Ink Spots and Louis and Ella and Mel Tormé. We know why we liked Glenn Miller better that Stan Kenton or vice versa. We know all the WWII buzz words like blitzkrieg, Luftwaffe, Spitfires, Mustangs, Zeros, Messerschmitts, Battle of the Bulge, Kamikazes, Iwo Jima, U-boats, Dunkirk, the Flying Tigers and hundreds more. We recall the shock of hearing Clark Gable say the word "damn" in "Gone With the Wind" (perhaps sadly comparing it to Demi Moore in the 1997 movie *G.I. Jane,* telling her drill sergeant, "Suck my dick!" with few in the audience being shocked). We remember that Betty Grable married Harry James. We remember Judy Garland and Mickey Rooney in the "Andy Hardy" series, and not from watching "Nick At Night." We also know too much about hair loss and arthritis and the trauma of aging, but that's not what we talk about here. This is a place for remembering, not so much for how it actually was, but for how it now seems to have been. This place is a time warp where yesteryear still breathes. If you're in luck, there is a place like it near where you live.

> *Memories are hunting horns*
> *Whose sound dies on the wind.*
> —GUILLAUME APOLLINAIRE (1880-1918)

Those who are over sixty and retired not only live in a world of "Who are you?" but also in a world of "Who were you?" The latter is okay if you are looking for friends with whom to share common interests; not okay if the intent is one-upsmanship. Once retired, admirals and seamen, generals and privates, bosses and workers, all share similar rank. Of course money is still important, but health is more important, and health does not defer to social standing.

> *This is the truth the poet sings,*
> *That a sorrow's crown of sorrow is remembering*

*happier things.*

—ALFRED LORD TENNYSON, *Locksley Hall* (1842)

We did not walk for exercise way back then; we walked because that was the way to get from one place to another. To get to school each morning I walked a mile to the trolley line where I waited, then paid a nickel for the ten-mile ride up the hill to my school. Jogging was for horses. Individual memories make us individuals; joint memories make us contemporaries. When you and I remember similar things we connect. Whatever our differences, we can share our history and our mortality. I walked a mile to school; you walked a mile to school. Kids today are too soft, right? Right.

*History is the essence of innumerable biographies.*

—THOMAS CARLYLE (1795-1881)

We and our contemporaries know what history is. History is Teddy Roosevelt, Lincoln, the Civil War, Jefferson, Washington and Christopher Columbus. History is not FDR or Give 'em Hell Harry. History is what happened before we were born. The kids think history is W.W.II and Korea. They are wrong. W.W.II and Korea are still very

much alive. We were there, so W.W.II can't really be history
. . . not quite yet.

*In memory, everything seems to happen to music.*

—TENNESSEE WILLIAMS (1911-83)

"You must remember this, A kiss is still a kiss, A sigh is still
a sigh. The world will always welcome lovers, As time goes
by," so sang Sam in *Casablanca,* and those of us who heard
it for the first time were almost as moved as we are hearing
it again for the umpteenth time. All those songs from the
movies, Broadway, the big bands and the jazz bands, our
own special music, is still lingering on old, brittle 78-rpm's,
on the LP albums in their fading dust jackets, on tape and
cassettes and now even on bright shiny new CDs, proving
that at least some of our music has staying power and
has been able to survive all the assorted technological
re-inventions. Also, a number of tasteful present-day artists
have seen fit to record their own versions of the standards:
Natalie Cole singing a duet with dead dad Nat. Which
brings up another distinction of note: we are the first gener-
ations to be entertained in (virtual) person by our deceased
heroes. Singers, dancers, actors, musicians, are all captured
by the camera and the microphone to endlessly repeat their

best performances, to become life-everlasting entertainment history. They say Elvis isn't dead? They're right!

*To me, old age is always fifteen years older than I am.*

—BERNARD BARUCH (1870-1965)

## A LETTER NEVER SENT

*Dear Georgie:*

*Even though you don't like me to mention it, you are five years and three days older than I am. It's nice having you out front there leading the parade with me in the middle and Alice Carol tagging along another seven years behind. We are siblings, but with the great gaps of time between us, we also have something of the "only child" about us, especially me, the only boy. Our memories often don't quite jibe. Our perspectives differ. We can look at the same things, things we all experienced in the past, and come up with differing testimony. We even see our parents through visions altered by age and time. Now, one thing we share is that we are all over sixty (two of us well over); members of that club. I'm sure that each one of us felt as we passed fifty-five that we had accomplished something, because mother died at fifty-five. And as we crossed sixty-six (not AC, yet), another mark, this one for Dad.*

*It is a strange feeling to be older than both your parents. We see them still with young eyes. We don't get to talk about this much because we are far flung and too much time passes between visits. Three children of proud parents, who have given them grandchildren and great-grandchildren they never knew. This is nothing very special, of course. It's the normal course of events. It is who almost all of us are.*

*Your Loving Brother*

*PS When the last 78-rpm turntable has rusted tight, will there still be music on those dusty records? As technology strides ahead, what is it leaving behind?*

❦

# AGE DISCRIMINATION

*There was an old woman tossed up in a basket,*
*Seventeen times as high as the moon;*
*And where she was going, I couldn't but ask her,*
*For under her arm, she carried a broom.*

(If she had been a 23-year-old *Sports Illustrated* swimsuit
model instead of an old woman, they never would
have tossed her up there is the first place.)

A ge discrimination occurs at all ages. In most school
districts you can't get into kindergarten until you
are five. And as we proceed through grammar and
high school years we are segregated by our class, which
mostly means by age. Parents don't like their daughters dat-
ing "older" boys (wisely). And when we finally reach the
job market we often fail to get a position because we are
"too young and inexperienced." Is it any wonder then that
age discrimination exists and continues to be a factor when
we reach our sixties—we were all taught to do it in school!
As an interesting aside, I can't help but wonder about the

law that prohibits anyone from running for the U.S. presidency until he or she is thirty-five years old. If an otherwise qualified 34-year-old wanted to run why couldn't he or she successfully claim age discrimination? Another interesting example is when I had just turned sixty-five I was quite sick with an undetermined lung disorder. At one point the specialist who was attempting to treat me said that what I probably needed to save my life was a lung transplant. "However," he added before I could even consider that possibility, "We don't perform them on anyone over sixty." Why? Probably just not enough years left to go to all that trouble and expense, especially when younger patients are in need. The same rule (if it is a rule) probably applies to all organ transplants and, I recently heard, even dialyses is not available to over sixty-five's. Not enough machines to go around, I suppose, but, HEY! what about the "Golden Years?" We bust our butts to get there and then some committee composed of younger doctors decides they can't spare a lung or a liver for the old folks. If that's not age discrimination, what is it? Sue the bastards, I say.

*I don't want to be horny when I'm seventy,*
*because it'll be so hard to fulfill. I mean, trying to*
*pick up some girl when you're seventy is difficult.*

—NEIL SIMIAN, *Playboy* (1979) (born July 4, 1927)

The first time I noticed anything different, I was walking down a New York City sidewalk glancing, as usual, at any and all exceptional young females coming toward me. I had just turned fifty and I had been looking at girls like this since puberty (like every other heterosexual male, admit it or not). What was different was that the girls had all of a sudden, it seemed, stopped looking back. My metamorphosis had taken place so subtly I had been caught unaware. Eye contact one moment, no eye contact the next. My time of hunkism, if it ever had existed except in my own mind, was over and my sexual allure was apparently now as dead and dry as the trickling sand in an hour glass. Youth, in our world, equals physical beauty and by the time any of us reaches sixty, youth is something we can no longer claim. The only consolation is that we are all, man or woman, straight or gay, locked into similar scenarios. That is why we tell each other, "Hey, you haven't changed a bit." Yeah, yeah. Back atcha.

> *Most people my age are dead.*
> —remark made by CASY STENGEL, (1890-1975)

But we are not dead (yet), we are just as alive as ever and that goes for most healthy over-sixty-ites. So we start looking around and we see that there are plenty of people who are also no longer young and all of a sudden we find ourselves making eye contact again. We have rediscovered our contemporaries. We have found the world of AARP and if you haven't, not to worry, AARP will find you. Ready or not, we have become members of an elite and growing power block. Just like back in high school, we are the seniors once again and nobody better mess with us.

*The (15th) Amendment nullifies sophisticated as well as simple-minded modes of discrimination.*

—FELIX FRANKFURTER,
U.S. Supreme Court Justice (1882-1965)

At one time I held a job which required me to hire and fire people "under" me. One day I was called to a meeting by some people "over" me. Actually, these people were on an equal par with me except for the fact that they represented management, which gave them a distinct advantage. Their message was as simple as it was alarming: Reduce your staff by three people. Submit the names and positions of these people within one week. Bam! I went back to my office in shock. I considered the people I worked with to be friends and colleagues. Besides, I needed them. What to do? Ever the loyal employee, I submitted my list within a week's time. It consisted of one female, 68 years old; one male 67; one female, pregnant. Almost immediately my presence was "requested" at another meeting and I learned (to my astonishment?) that my selection was unsatisfactory. It seems there were certain anti-discrimination laws to be taken into consideration. I stuck by my guns—these were the only three I could spare. The upshot was a compromise. I didn't have to fire anybody, but I would have to lose three people by attrition: the next three employees that left of their own accord could not be replaced. At this point in time, I can't really remember whether anyone ever left of their own accord or not.

*Age and treachery will triumph over youth and skill.*

—ANON.

The face cream commercials on TV and in magazines are fascinating. They almost invariably show a model who might be as much as thirty years old as proof that their product can keep a person's skin from "aging." At seventy years old it is easily possible to have a thirty-year-old granddaughter. (If you had your first child at 17 and your child and her child did the same, when you are 68 years old your daughter would be 51, your granddaughter, 34 and your great granddaughter, 17.) We view the years from thirty to forty as the mellowing of youth, not the beginnings of old age. Where are the face creams for the over-sixty set? In fact where are the over-sixty people in the commercials? We see them in health insurance ads, once in a while in a pricey car ad, and in commercials for arthritis medications, dentures and extra-absorbent undergarments. We see ourselves impersonated by youthful models with white hair. Publications or TV programs which have an older audience have trouble attracting advertisers. Older readership or viewer-ship is considered a stigma by Madison Avenue. Why? I don't pretend to understand it. I know for a fact that my wife and I spend more money than our offspring for a vast variety of products. Wake up, Mad. Ave. We're for real. We're spenders and we are hanging around longer than ever. We don't react well to discriminatory treatment, and we don't like being ignored.

*Hey, Pops, you still got your moves.*

—ANON.
(Comment shouted at me in New York City as I sprinted across the street to beat a red light. I was sixty years old, and no one had ever called me "Pops" before.)

## A LETTER NEVER SENT

*Dear Skip:*

*Since you have always been a "discriminating" individual it occurred to me to broach this subject with you in hopes of assuaging some of the no doubt many lingering guilt feelings you must have hoarded away about your treatment of all of us less lofty than yourself (now you know I'm just fooling, here). When we speak of age discrimination we are talking of discrimination against the aged. While this is certainly a legitimate topic, let's consider a different perspective, discrimination by the aged. All of us over-sixty types have come from a time period, in our youth, when discrimination of all stripes was so rampant that many of us didn't even realize it existed. True, none of us were slave holders because Honest Abe and a lot of dead Union soldiers had put an end to that before we were born. But in the South the color line was still intact (separate public facilities for everything), women could vote but were restricted in many other areas and so forth. (By the way were you aware that many women suffragists did not support the 15th amendment that gave black males voting rights because women still couldn't vote? Women had to wait for the 19th amendment in 1920.) Do older folks as a group resent the more open society in which they now find themselves? Well,* the answer is "No," not as a group anyway. I, for one, am proud that this country continues to try to make everyone equal and free under the law. On the other hand I know plenty of old-dog, hard-core types that cling to the past and long for days of yore. Not you, Skip, and not me. As for the discriminators, time will soon take care of them.

*Your Friend*

# LOVE

*Curlylocks, Curlylocks,*
*Wilt thou be mine?*
*Thou shalt not wash dishes*
*Nor yet feed the swine,*
*But sit on a cushion*
*And sew a fine seam,*
*And feed upon strawberries,*
*Sugar and cream.*

(Love is so simple in the beginning, but later on, when you can no longer see well enough to sew a fine seam, and when your diet precludes sugar and cream, there's still enough love left to wash the dishes, feed the pigs and not complain.)

L ove is that mystical something that we can't turn on or off. Instead, it mysteriously turns us on or off. Some love is fleeting, some lasting. But we all love someone or other most of the time, and we hope that that someone loves us back. Even when we are not in a relationship, we feel love when we hear certain music, watch certain films, go by certain places, dream certain dreams. Love is simply an integral part of each human being, and it can be over-powering. It is with us at birth and, with any luck at all, with us at death. Love ebbs and flows like the sea, like a great symphony, and when it wells up within us, we usually surrender to it. Love for those of us over sixty is as meaningful and significant as at any other time in our lives. Love for the elderly may not be as much of a white hot flame as it once was, but it is baked in deep enough to survive a cold spell.

> *I long to walk with some old lover's ghost,*
> *Who died before the god of love was born.*
>
> —JOHN DONNE, *Love's Diety* (1572-1631)

How much can one person care for another person? Physically we are all entities with our self-contained body vessels requiring individual feedings, fluids, medications and the rest. Hit your thumb with a hammer and it is not felt across the room. Sprain an ankle and no one limps but you. And yet, as John Donne famously observed,("No man is an island"), we are connected with our fellow humans in many and complicated ways and the ultimate connection is called love.

*Oh, the days dwindle down to a precious few,*
*September, November!*
*And these few precious days I'll spend with you.*
*These precious days, I'll spend with you.*

—Maxwell Anderson, *September Song,* song lyric (1938)

Diamonds and gold are precious because the supply is limited. For most of us, as our days dwindle our love grows; the fewer days, the more precious. Those of us who have been married for many years find ourselves in a strangely terrifying duet. The handsome couple that exchanged vows in its youth has changed drastically. Each has watched the other bend to time. All those years. All those moments. The once young beauty with the perfect female form has been transformed. The youthful, handsome groom, muscular and agile, has evolved. Our physical replacements are strangers who resemble our own grandparents, aged aunts and uncles, people we never quite believed we would ever become. Yet here we are holding on to one another, kissing fondly, complaining softly, secretly wondering when death will come undo the knot that has bound us together for so long.

*Change partners and dance with me.*

—Irving Berlin, *Change Partners,* song lyric (1937 )

Not all of us have enjoyed enduring relationships. Many of us have loved more than once if not frequently. There are manifold examples of young/old relationships. The old "fool" with the ambitious bimbo. The grand dame with the gigolo. But love the second, fourth or sixth time around is still love or such a reasonable facsimile that those involved can't seem to tell the difference. Advanced years do not prevent us from being tempted by the young and beautiful all around us. Some resist, others cannot.

> *Old as I am, for ladies' love unfit,*
> *The power of beauty I remember yet.*

—JOHN DRYDEN, *Fables Ancient and Modern* (1700)

As we drift off to sleep at night we seem to exist, in that twilight moment, only in our minds and we are of no particular age. In fact we can be any age we choose and we do not often choose old. There we can meet again former intimate friends and there we can recreate good times. Bad moments from the past can be resurrected and set aright. Haunting failures can become passionate successes. High school romancers may be summoned still youthful to touch us tenderly and gaze at us with love because, in our mind's eye, we too are once again young and smooth. And that attractive person who waited on our table at lunch today may well come to knock upon our door, enter our room and hold us seductively, and for that lovely, fictious, sensual moment rejuvenate us.

> *Our summer day,*
> *withers away,*
> *too soon, too soon.*

—OGDEN NASH, *Speak Low*, song lyric (1943)

People love people, but people also love many other things. People love animals: dogs, cats, pigs, dolphins, whales and elephants. The dogs and cats thrive on this love, but the wild beasts have a problem sharing the same planet with humans because humans love their own kind best. Take this test: Would you kill the last tiger on Earth to save your grandchild? You would because you would be compelled to. Our family ties are stronger than our objectivity. We might feel that the last tiger on Earth is more important than the life of yet another human, but love overtakes our perspective and we simply must protect and preserve our own. We can find solace in the certainty that, had the roles been reversed, the tiger would have behaved similarly. We all are compelled to protect our own, tigers as well as people. Love is not a whim; we have little choice but to obey its selfish commands.

*Sir, more than kisses, letters mingle souls;*
*For, thus friends absent speak.*

—JOHN DONNE "To Sir Henry Wotton" (1633)

"My Darling . . . I feel your presence near me as surely as
the warmth from the fire, and yet to touch you is impossible like reaching, groping for something in the black emptiness of night knowing that which you seek is not there but
hoping, hoping, hoping that by some strange act of fate it
may be because you cannot see and are not sure." This my
wife to be (Anne Freeze, 23 years old)) wrote to me on
February 1, 1954 (air mail, six cents), during an extended
separation when I was in the USAF. How do I know her
exact words? Because I saved the letter and it means as
much to me now as it did the day I received it. When we
were young lovers and apart we wrote each other daily.
Today I frequently use e-mail, often the phone, but still
nothing compares to letter writing. You say e-mail is letter
writing? Sort of, but it's not really the same. Real letters
come from someplace deeper. E-mail may be kept for a
week or a month but then it gets the delete button. Phone
calls are merely for the moment. But letters, especially love
letters, are kept, treasured like locks of hair and fading photographs. The paper was touched by the writers; the words

were directly applied. The old letters reside deep inside drawers, in attic boxes. His letters are bundled with her letters. They keep asking, "Do you love me?" And answering, "Yes, I do!" The words are as fresh as the day they were written. The lovers no longer exist.

> *I remember every little thing you used to do*
> *I'm so lonely,*
> *'Lover, come back to me!'*

> —OSCAR HAMMERSTEIN II,
> *Lover, Come Back To Me*, song lyric (1928)

### A LETTER NEVER SENT

*Dearest Anne:*

*The things we know now that we didn't know then. Had we known them, what would it have changed? Probably very little. Yet in our ignorance or wisdom we hung together through it all to reach this point. There are the scars that will never heal that we set aside, someplace. There are your scars, my scars and our scars. We do our best not to dwell on them. We have each other and even though we are different people now than those two enraptured young sweethearts who met forty-five years ago, we are the result of them. Species evolve.*

*Individuals evolve. Some of the fight has gone out of us, but none of the love. Young lovers expect perfection. Old lovers understand imperfection. We understand each other so much better now. We are determined to enjoy the time left to us. We are devoted and loyal. We are supporters and defenders of each other. We are so close it is inconceivable that we are separate, but of course we are. Together in the same vehicle, we zoom down the same treacherous road, enjoying the last part of our ride even more than the first. Hang on!*

*Your Loving Husband*

# DYING AND DEATH

*All the birds of the air*
*Fell a-sighing and a-sobbing,*
*When they heard the bell toll*
*For poor Cock Robin.*

(Death always leaves a void, even when it's only a boid.)

After living sixty or sixty-five years people start doing weird things. They tend to move around a lot. Many buy and use house trailers and motor homes, enduring cramped conditions to seek new horizons. Mostly what they find is other trailer types and they compare notes. Some seniors choose ocean cruises with similar results. Still others devise various forms of travel to see the world or the country "while still young enough to enjoy it." Many, if not most, hike, walk, swim, jog, cycle, climb, swing golf clubs or tennis racquets or fly rods. The shared desire seems to be to achieve a state of almost perpetual motion. Action symbolizes life. Death is such a very long stillness. There seems to be a grim universal blind hope that it will be harder for the death dart to hit a moving target.

*There is no cure for birth and death save to enjoy the interval.*

—GEORGE SANTAYANA,
"Soliloquies in England and Later Soliloquies". (1922)

Case #1—Sometimes death is a surprise. She was going along pretty good. She was being useful, helpful, unselfish. She had nothing but love in her heart for all mankind. And, she was taking good care of herself. For breakfast she ate bran cereal with sliced banana, no sugar, skim milk. No coffee. Glass of squeezed orange. She walked two miles and her legs and lungs felt strong. She looked at her husband of forty-five years and knew that their love for each other had only increased over that time. Her children were doing well and they had brought her three wonderful grand kids. The sun was shining as she lay down for a short nap that was to last for all eternity. There wasn't one person who knew her who didn't say or think, "What a shock. So sudden."

*Golden lads and girls all must,*
*As chimny-sweepers, come to dust*

—WILLIAM SHAKESPEARE, *Cymbeline* (1609-10)

Case #2—Sometimes death is anticipated. Dying is an earthward process. First he had to give up jogging because of his knees. Eventually he had them replaced, but one of the operations was less than successful. Then he slipped on a newly mopped floor in the supermarket, and busted his hip. He wasn't seventy yet, too young for this crap. They put a pin in his hip but that didn't work out either and he and his devoted wife were dealing with a walker (that he used less and less) and a wheel chair (that he used more and more). With the reduced mobility he, who had always been so active, never seemed to feel exactly well. His energy was gone. His desires, sexual and otherwise, were gone. He wanted to feel better, but that seemed to occupy all of his thinking. It wasn't long before he had his first stroke. Therapy for stroke victims is difficult and calls for dedication, hard work, mental toughness. He seemed to stop caring. His right side was mostly paralyzed and he had trouble forming words and even thinking of once familiar phrases. He pretty much stopped communicating. Three months later he had his second stroke and three weeks after that it was all over. There wasn't one person who knew him who didn't say or think, "It's for the best. Now he can rest in peace."

*After sixty years the stern sentence of the burial service seems*
*to have a meaning that one did not notice in former years.*
*There begins to be something personal about it.*

—OLIVER WENDELL HOLMES (1809-94)

The thing is, we don't really get to choose between Case
#1 and Case #2. Fate chooses for us. We can attempt to
impact our physical well being by following "doctor's
orders" and what we learn from reading and watching, and
talking with friends and associates, but our genes are pretty
much in place and whatever future medical miracles are
coming in that area will not be in time for us. A glance at
the obit page offers the obvious clue that there is no
escape. So like lambs being led to slaughter, we bide our
time, wait patiently and, in most cases, bravely, for the
inevitable. We even joke about it. We attend the funerals of
friends and family. We weep and then we laugh. We proceed because proceeding everyday, day by day, is what
human beings on the planet Earth in the Twentieth Century
have got to do. It's that one law of nature we cannot seem
to alter.

*We are the Dead. Short days ago*
*We lived, felt dawn, saw sunset glow,*

*Loved and were loved, and now we lie*
*In Flanders fields.*

—COLONEL JOHN MCCRAE, *In Flanders Fields* (1872-1918)

When you top sixty and begin your perilous journey toward those bigger, scarier numbers, you begin to focus on the reality of your own demise and you may, at times, be quite overcome with self pity. At such moments I find it helpful to remember the fields of crosses and other markers in various parts of the world that represent young service people who left life early on the battlefields attempting to preserve the freedoms we enjoy today. They made it possible for us to experience sixty and beyond and to leave children and grandchildren. The young fighters died knowing only their youth, but also believing that there was no other way to preserve our precious way of life than to place themselves in harm's way. I think, if these young people had the courage to give up their lives, then who am I to be afraid now having lived life to its fullest? I am grateful to them and filled with awe at their sacrifice.

*But at my back I always hear*
*Time's winged chariot hurrying near;*

*And yonder all before us lie*
*Deserts of vast eternity.*

—ANDREW MARVELL, *To His Coy Mistress* (1650-52)

He wanted to have his ashes scattered in the northern
Virginia woods; across Long Island's beautiful Great Peconic
Bay; on the ski slopes of a special Colorado mountainside;
along Maine's rough and rocky coast; over the saltwater flats
of Islamorada, all of the places where he had felt the closest
to nature, where his days had been full of meaning and joy.
After his death he wanted to no longer take up space on
Earth even underground; he wanted to become Earth. That,
it seemed, would have to satisfy his desire for a taste of
immortality.

*That's all there is, there isn't anymore.*

—ETHEL BARRYMORE (1879-1959)

It's going to happen, we all know it. But is that any reason
to be obsessed with death? As the saying goes, we're going
to be dead a long, long time, so if we must be obsessed
with something it would seem to make more sense to be
obsessed with life. Some consider life to be short and
sweet. Others believe it to be long and arduous. Actually,

while life can seem long and arduous, the short, sweet moments can make it all worthwhile.

> *There are too many people in this country*
> *who think that dying is an option.*

> —DR. NANCY SNYDERMAN,
> on *Good Morning America* (1997)

If they find the cures for all the various cancers there would certainly be cause for justifiable celebration. But eliminating one way to go, and a nasty way it can be, has absolutely nothing to do with eliminating death. Prolonging life is merely procrastinating death. What is a natural life span? If they do away with strokes and heart attacks and AIDS and lung, liver and kidney failures, death will still be there. If they ban guns and knives and poisons and bombs, death may wait, but not forever. If they stop all car accidents, snake bites, starvation, leaps from tall buildings, murders and hangings, it will make little difference in the long run. What begins, must end. What emerges from the nether world for its Earthly visitation, must, sooner or later, move on. Life often feeds on death, but death always has the last bite.

*They all go into the dark, but their cars stay in the garage.*

—JAMES ATLAS, *The New Yorker* (1997)

While death must be considered one of the most serious of all subjects, there is actually a great deal of humor surrounding it. This reflects the resilience of the human spirit, courage in the face of annihilation. It's called gallows humor. When they were young, Robert Benchley and Dorothy Parker of Algonquin round table fame, spent some time writing funny lines for tombstones. Two of the best were "This One Is On Me" and "Pardon My Dust." I found what I consider to be a good line for my own headstone on a tag attached to a pair of socks I purchased at a factory outlet store: "Slightly Imperfect."

> *Do not go gentle into that good night*
> *Old age should burn and rage at close of day;*
> *Rage, rage against the dying of the light.*

—DYLAN THOMAS,
*Do Not Go Gentle Into That Good Night* (1953)

For the most part, our children and grandchildren want us to hang on as long as possible, and we try to do that until something happens in our minds that tells us it's time to move on. At that moment our offspring represent a future that no longer includes us. Our thoughts turn backwards and we think of our mothers and fathers and friends who are dead but not gone from our minds. The living mix with the dead as we hallucinate. This brings great fear to our children, great peace to us.

*Grandfather, you were the pillar of fire in front of the camp, and now we are just a camp left alone in the dark; and we are so cold and sad.*

—NOA BEN-ARTZI, upon the death of her grandfather, Israeli Prime Minister Yitzhak Rabin (1995)

Your death, my death, will leave behind an emptiness for those still living who loved us. They can dial the same number as usual; there will be no answer, ever. They will have to continue on without us to find their own destinies. Will we be together in death as we were in life? No living person knows, no dead person will tell. I think often about my parents, long gone, but still clearly envisioned in my mind. I recreate the death of my 35-year-old son over and over, changing nothing. I count the years since his departure, years that mean nothing to him, but seem unreal to me. Death is permanent. The most we can hope to do is to prepare for death while we are alive so that our loved ones remaining on Earth will best be able to cope with the rest of their own lives. There is no proof that we will not all be together again. Something to cling to.

*There is no longer a necessary reason for me being.*
*Already the long shadows of untimely oblivion*
*creep over me, and I shall decrease forever.*

—RALPH WALDO EMERSON (1802-83)

Given enough time, we come to understand how much time is finally enough. When your world shrinks down and you are your own last contemporary, your moment has arrived.

*Under the wide and starry sky,*
*Dig the grave and let me lie.*
*Glad did I live and gladly die,*
*And laid me down with a will.*

*This be the verse you grave for me:*
*Here he lies where he longed to be;*
*Home is the sailor, home from the sea,*
*And the hunter home from the hill.*

—ROBERT LOUIS STEVENSON, *Requiem* (1850-1894)

## A LETTER NEVER SENT

Dear Paul:

Remember when Jim gaffed his wife in her leg by mistake and, being a doctor, was able to patch her up, and being a totally possessed big-game fisherman, was able to convince her to continue trolling and not go back home? The time she had her gall bladder out Jim told me, "We got the bladder but left in the gall." I think, however, he was the one with the gall. Guts, too. Died in the fighting chair with a huge blue marlin on the other end of his line. Probably the way you would have preferred to go. Where did you go, Paul? No one savored life's rich flavor more. You were brave and bright and able and a companion for all trips. You were a sportsman: a hunter of ducks, a fisher of ocean swimmers from secret places. Especially, like Jim, those marlin in the Gulf off South Pass. But so many other fish in so many other places, too. Like others of your ilk (a much maligned community nowadays) you were in touch with the natural world and were able to see what the self-righteous non-sporting folk were doing to it with their developments and malls. Back when you were here there seemed to be plenty of room for man and nature to co-exist, but now the human's have taken over. At the same time they malign the hunters for their one-at-a-time kills, they bulldoze *malign the hunters for their one-at-a-time kills, they bulldoze and pave over entire forests, wiping out the natural popula- tions. Where have you gone, Paul? Where ever it is, I think it quite possible that our entire species may be joining you soon.*

*Your Friend*

❧

# ONE MORE TIME

*An itsy, bitsy spider went up the water spout,*
*Down came the rain and washed the spider out.*
*Out came the sun and dried up all the rain,*
*And the itsy, bitsy spider went up the spout again.*

(We all want another chance. Who knows—next time we
might not get washed out the spout?)

Every fisherman wants one more cast before heading
for the dock. That is, after he makes his final toss
and reels back his lure, he will invariably say, "Just
one more," as if somehow, this one last time, a monstrous,
record-breaking fish will miraculously grab hold. It's the
gambler's faulty instinct to believe that one more spin of
the wheel or toss of the dice will change everything. The
dream of winning the lottery, the hope of rectifying an
unrectifiable wrong, the longing for one more chance to get
it right; these frantic wishes are usually about as useful as a
drowning man bothering to come up for the third (and last)

time. The reality is, if you did gain the chance to revisit some awful past failure in your life you would still, in all likelihood, fail miserably one more time.

> *The Moving Finger writes; and, having writ,*
> *Moves on: nor all your Piety nor Wit*
> *Shall lure it back to cancel half a Line,*
> *Nor all your Tears wash out a Word of it*
>
> —OMAR KAYYÁM, *Rubáiyát*,(11-12th c.);
> Trans. Edward FitzGerald (1859)

At my age I am sometimes not in complete control of my mind. Sometimes we struggle (my mind and I) to see who is in charge. Sometimes my mind wants to think about things I would rather forget ever happened. These extemporaneous re-visitations can pop up completely out of context with the moment, say when I'm driving the car. With my wife at my side I am staring at the highway, paying attention to the job at hand when, oops, here comes that embarrassing time again to haunt me. I may utter a soft groan. My wife looks over. I say, "Nothing." She shrugs, looks away. My mind returns to the road. The ghosts recede.

*Play It Again, Sam.*

—WOODY ALLEN, film title (1969)
(Note: Neither Bogart nor Bergman ever said this exact
sequence of words in the film *Casablanca*.)

When I was in my first year as a newspaper reporter I had
occasion to talk with Garry Moore on the telephone. Garry
Moore was a major TV variety show host at that time who
introduced to the world, among other notables, Carol
Burnett. After I finished interviewing him about the perti-
nent subject, there was a pause. I had always had the idea
that I would like to break into TV comedy writing. It
sounded like a fun way to make a living. And, here I was,
with the man who could make it happen on the other end
of the line. "Uh, Mr. Moore," I ventured. "Yes?" Did he
sound rushed? He was a  busy man. Big television star. Had
I already taken up too much of his time? "Uh, well, nothing
more I guess. Thanks so much for talking with me." Click.
(Back to the present.) Dumb chicken-shit kid, says my
mind. Long time ago, get over it, I say back with a soft
audible groan. Wife looks over. "Nothing," I say.

*One more once.*

—COUNT BASIE, concert signature remark

What is eating a worm hole in your sub-conscious? What better-forgotten event crawls between your ears uninvited? A love lost because of a dumb move? A life lost because of some irresponsible act? Money lost because of a stupid investment? Money not gained because of no investment? A friendship lost because of some trivial misunderstanding? Even though these events may plague you, they are mostly irreversible. But since you lived them, they won't ever go all the way away until you do. You own them as much as you own your big toe, your pumping heart; as much as Custer owns Little Big Horn. At least he didn't have to spend half a lifetime reliving his failure.

> *Man is a history-making creature who can*
> *neither repeat his past nor leave it behind.*
> —D. H. LAWRENCE, *The Dyers Hand* (1962)

Sometimes, perhaps while driving, instead of a groan, there will be a soft smile as your memory replays an event from your past of which you can be justly proud. When I was in college I once saved a beautiful blond young woman from being raped by three drunken students. Her date had passed out; she had had too much to drink; they were intoxicated to the point where a very bad idea seemed like a very good idea. They had her down on the floor in an upstairs hallway where I came across them and was able to dissuade them (they were freshmen, I was a senior). I led the girl to the relative safety of my study room, where she could spend the rest of the night alone on my couch. I showed her how to bolt the door from the inside and I left her there. By the time I checked on her the next morning, she was gone. I sometimes wonder if she remembers the incident? Perhaps this moment I like to recall is one she keeps trying to forget.

*This only is denied even to God: the power to undo the past.*

—Aristotle, quoting Agathon
*Nicomachean Ethics* (4th c. B.C.)

While we are not yet wholly one with the past, our lives are mostly lived, which means that we are, now, mostly over. At sixty-plus we are but an accumulation of our past actions, the remnants of all our studies and stunts, victories and defeats. We are in all likelihood, beyond our last hurrah. We are a retired doctor in a comfy waterside nest or a retired (hopefully) murderer still on death row. We are a nurse who needs nursing, a flyer who is grounded, a leader looking for someone to follow. Of course, as long as we remain alive we ARE, but we keep edging ever closer to WERE. Newspaper obits are just so many little individual bites of history, but put them all together and they become the story of a town, a state, a country. Confronted with our lives mostly gone, we remain surprisingly hopeful. We are asked how we want to be remembered, but mostly we'll settle for just being remembered at all. When we vanish, we want to leave an echo. We can't do it over again ourselves, but we can continue to live vicariously through our descendants, our children, grandchildren, great-grandchildren. These are our ambassadors to the future. If they remember us, then they represent us. One more time? Hell, maybe more than just once.

*encore*: . . . *a demand for repetition or reappearance* . . .
—*Webster's New Collegiate Dictionary*

## A LETTER NEVER SENT

*Dear Dick:*
*If I had it to do over again would I have irrevocably cut off our friendship? Knowing me, under the same circumstances, probably; which is not to say I don't harbor any regrets. Which is*

*not to say should my phone ring right now and I answer to find you on the line, that I would not say please let's forgive and forget. Where are you? How are you? How is Connie? Which is not to say that this imagined conversation isn't bringing a tear to my eye. Because in the face of eternity, perspectives change and the previously unforgivable sin becomes a minor misdemeanor, nothing more than a petty, peevish complaint. The vision of two minnows viciously fighting each other as they are about to be gobbled by a great white shark comes to mind. If I knew where you were in this world—if I knew if you were in this world—I would call right now, because we were close friends, and as we age close friends become a scarce, rare, diminishing commodity. Maybe I will try to find you. In fact, if you are somewhere, Dick, and you read this, call me. How good it would be to talk about some of the old times. Even though we cannot change a past grievance, we can often ignore it, belittle it, move on.*

*Your Former (and future?) Friend*

# EPILOGUE

*Never trust anyone under sixty.*

—ANON

For some time now this book has been my friend and confidant. I am sorry to bid it farewell. What I said in the Prologue was not exactly true—that I wrote it just to impress my family. The truer reason is that I felt guilty about taking up space on this planet for the dubious purpose of breathing in and out, eating, excreting and mowing the grass. I felt I had to contribute as best I could to my time. I had to try to leave my little nail scratches on the Earth's surface. I had to keep on clawing, keep the words coming, on the chance that something worthwhile might eventually emerge. Nothing earthshaking, mind you, but my own take on how things are.

As noted previously, the subjects we ponder in this book are as old as mankind and, as the quotes prove, the unanswered questions remain pretty much the same. But civilization forges on and the hints we can even now see of what the future may bring are as amazing as they are frightening. We are zooming off into space, cloning animals, reproducing ourselves at an alarming rate, creating life in the laboratory, extending the lives of individual humans and moving rapidly ahead on a vast number of scientific and technological fronts. What will the future bring? The list of possibilities ranges from total extermination of all human life to the eventual expansion of mankind throughout the universe. None of us will be around to learn the eventualities but most of us can glean some satisfaction from knowing that whatever human destiny may turn out to be, we played our part.

*It is a mistake to look too far ahead. Only one link
in the chain of destiny can be handled at a time.*

—SIR WINSTON CHURCHILL, speech (1945)

Turning sixty is a beginning not an end. Every day you are alive deserves the best that you can give it and having given, the day will return to you benefits. Youth is a wonderful place and we have been there; had our allotted time there. But sixties, seventies, eighties and beyond are also decades of life to be explored and valued.

We are conditioned by our busy pasts to visualize enjoyment as a weekend at the beach with a good book. A time to "un-lax" as we used to call it. I guess that word meant a time to let the stress gush out like the air rushing from an over-inflated inner tube. Tension was so much a part of our daily lives then, and now, all at once we confront empty days and total deflation. A weekend or a week at the beach with a good book is fine, but with months and years of free time staring us in the face our inner tube quickly goes flat, the paperback plots run together like so much gibberish and we are in serious need of a touch of stress just to keep us regular.

What to do? That question has as many answers as there are people who face it. The choice is up to the individual—you. What do you know how to do? Free time probably won't turn a retired shoe salesman into a librarian, though that's not impossible. In fact post employment education is popular and pays big benefits in self esteem and mental growth. And growth, expansion, improvement are the kinds of results that will lead to self assuredness and toughness needed to deal with life after sixty. Shrinkage is your enemy. Growth is your friend.

Another enemy is idleness. Stick this simple motto up on your refrigerator door: "Keep Busy." (Watching TV is not keeping busy.) If your mobility is limited you can read. Learn to draw and paint. Play the kazoo. Do crosswords. The object is to keep those little gray cells challenged and in motion.

For those of you who are not conversant with computers, my advice is to drop everything and learn how now. There is no shortage of classes to teach you the skills. Every town in America of any size at all has a computer store. Just look in the yellow pages. See if you can find a small shop rather than one of the big chains. Talk to the people and get their advice on which computer to buy because they will be your teacher.

Then go to the chain stores if necessary to save a buck. You can get everything you need for under $1000. Buy the computer first, then the lessons. You can't learn to play the piano without a piano. You will use your computer every day for corresponding with friends via e-mail, for poking about on the internet and for a long list of other activities that will make you happy, confident and feel like you're on the cutting edge.

With an aging body infirmities will eventually come . Don't dwell on this, but do plan on it. Discuss it with your close family. Develop a strategy. It will help give all of you peace of mind.

People die at all ages, children most tragically. Who knows when that unseen truck will come bearing down. People in their thirties and forties have strokes, heart attacks, cancer. So in that regard seventy is no different than fifty. Concentrate on living, not dying, and your life will be the better for it. And, concentrate on loving too and your world after 60 will be a warmer and more wonderful place.

*A baby is God's opinion that life should go on.*

—CARL SANDBURG (1948)